LEADING
WOMEN
TO THE
HEART
OF
GOD

LEADING
WOMEN
TO THE
HEART
OF
GOD

CREATING A DYNAMIC
WOMEN'S MINISTRY

LYSA TERKEURST
GENERAL EDITOR

MOODY PRESS
CHICAGO

All Scripture quotations, unless otherwise indicated, are taken from the *Holy Bible, New International Version®*. NIV®. Copyright © 1973, 1978, 1984 by International Bible Society. Used by permission of Zondervan Publishing House. All rights reserved.

Scripture quotations marked NASB are taken from the *New American Standard Bible®*, © Copyright The Lockman Foundation 1960, 1962, 1963, 1968, 1971, 1972, 1973, 1975, 1977, 1995. Used by permission.

Cover Photography: © 2002 Nancy Brown/ImageBank

Library of Congress Cataloging-in-Publication Data

Leading women to the heart of God / Lysa TerKeurst, general editor.
    p. cm.
    Includes bibliographical references.
    ISBN 0-8024-4920-4
    1. Church work with women. 2. Women in church work. I. TerKeurst, Lysa.
BV4445 .L43 2002
259'.082 5--dc 21

2002008165

3 5 7 9 10 8 6 4

Printed in the United States of America

*I dedicate this book
to every woman who has a desire
to make a difference for Christ
in her sphere of influence.
May God inspire and encourage you through this book.*

CONTENTS

PART FOUR
EXPANDING A WOMEN'S MINISTRY

PART FIVE
MAINTAINING A WOMEN'S MINISTRY

FOREWORD

What is a man doing writing the foreword to a leadership book for women? Well, there are several reasons. My mom was a delightful Christian wife and mother. I married a very special lady to whom I owe just about everything. And for more than three decades I served as pastor to some of the most wonderful, godly women in the world. But you want to know the main reason I agreed to write these words? I believe that women —ladies like you—are crucial to successful Christian homes, vibrant churches, and a redeemed society.

George Barna has written, "Women more often than not take the lead role in the spiritual life of the family. Women emerge as the primary—or only—spiritual mentor and role model for family members."

In a fairly recent survey the Barna Research Group found that for 80 percent the word "spiritual" described women accurately. Seventy percent of those ladies questioned resonated to the phrase "deeply spiritual." These findings rank much higher than men do when the same questions were asked, 63 percent and 50 percent. In addition, it is documented that one-half of all women desired to be personally active in the church, compared to just 36 percent of men.[1]

Now, do I find great comfort in those figures? Not really! I long for and have given my life to encourage men to accept their God-given places of Christian leadership. Perhaps in time they will. We are seeing little hints of progress, but the truth is that in most homes, and in a large number of churches, you ladies are the catalyst for the development of Christian maturity in our society. I know you don't like to hear those things—but it's the truth.

I have prayed and taught men for years that if they would assume their biblical role the church would be revived and many of society's ills would find healing. I am still praying and teaching. You ladies are key to all of this. Especially as you challenge the men in your lives to "step up" and take the lead. Yet I return to the facts—without you ladies living the life of Christ and remaining faithful to the call of God in your lives, the church would be only a shadow of what it is today. Thank you.

In churches I was privileged to pastor, we attempted to do several things in ministry to our ladies so that they might involve themselves in meaningful programs and opportunities.

We encouraged fellowship and provided nurture. We taught our women how to pray and offered them the example of godly role models. We equipped them with tools to be the wives and mothers God intended and challenged them to use their gifts and graces for the work of the church. We put great emphasis upon the total person's developing spiritually, emotionally, and physically.

The response was gratifying. In every church there was always a team of godly women who exhibited a variety of gifts and talents and who would come forward and give leadership to our women's ministry. I valued their willingness to be used.

Perhaps as you read these words you are one of those ladies who has given and given to your local church ministry. You're tired. You're overwhelmed. You're weary in well doing. No wonder! Look at all you do, but also look at all God has been doing through you. Don't give up—please!

I will always remember a group of ladies in our church in Salem, Oregon, who began to believe God for something very special. They were moving beyond the ordinary in their commitment to women's ministry. They were taking a bold step to widen their influence.

A conference for women was proposed—called "Oasis." It was one of the first major conferences of its kind in the Northwest. Our sanctuary was turned into a tropical paradise complete with real waterfalls, palm trees, and beautiful flowers. It worked! Ladies came by the hundreds. Our ladies' efforts were rewarded. "Oasis" was a yearly event for more than a decade. Scores of women from every walk of life found renewal and hope because God saw fit to bless the faith of a few brave women. He will reward you in the same way. You never know where your dreams will take you. Don't ever stop dreaming. You, like new wine in new wineskins, are equipped as never before to make a difference in your home, your church, and your world.

Because you do so much, and are probably also often taken for granted, I doubt if you really understand just how crucial you are to the success of your local church. Don't give up. Your absence would leave an irreplaceable vacuum.

It would be very worthwhile as you read the following pages to let the words, like a mirror, reflect in your life. If you're tired, take a step back. Check your priorities and come back stronger. If you're discouraged, seek out one who will understand your concerns, and talk to him or her. If you're struggling spiritually, make it your goal to grow closer to your Lord. If you're overwhelmed as a wife and a mom, or your singleness is a painful reality, quiet yourself, and reflect on how much you are loved by the One who created you, and He will give you the strength you need for the journey and a way out of temptation. You are not required to be a super anything—just the person God called you to be.

I have often preached a sermon entitled "If Mama Ain't Happy, Ain't Nobody Happy." I found those words to be very true. We really want you to be happy. At our house for the longest time on our refrigerator door was a little square magnet. There were no pictures. We didn't put the stick figures of our grandchildren on display—just a single magnet that said "If Papa Ain't Happy, Ain't Nobody Cares!"

A little tongue-in-cheek perhaps, but we who have put this book together really do care about you. We want you to be fulfilled as a woman —a wife—a mother. We want you engaged in meaningful pursuits. We want you to grow spiritually, and be motivated to good works. From what we hear, that is what you want as well.

As you live in the pages of *Leading Women to the Heart of God,* we urge you to let the thoughts and ideas be blessed to your own heart by the Holy Spirit. If you are challenged, accept it. If you are confronted with a sin, confess it! If a flaw is exposed, don't ignore it. If a dream is ignited, follow it! I believe you're in for a very positive literary journey.

And now, what is a man doing writing the foreword to a leadership book for women? Because I think you are key to the revival in the church we have all been praying for and because I think this book, under the leadership of Lysa TerKeurst, could help change your life. And as George Barna says, "[You] women are the backbone of the Christian congregation in America." Happy reading!

> H. B. London Jr.
> Vice President, Ministry Outreach/Pastoral Ministries
> Focus on the Family

---

[1] *The Barna Update,* The Barna Research Group, 6 March 2000.

ACKNOWLEDGMENTS

Several years ago, God gave me the desire to start a revival in the hearts of women all across this country. I didn't know how something of this magnitude could be accomplished, but I knew if I walked in obedience, God would show me the way. I also knew He would bring other women with similar desires and dedication to join me on this journey. This book is one of the pieces God has put into place that I believe will fan the flames of revival.

First, a big thank you to all the contributing writers. You are godly women with God-sized visions and hearts sold out to the cause of Christ. Hats off to you, dear friends!

Yvette Maher—A special thank you for letting me spend

time with you and share my blue-sky dreams. Isn't God amazing . . . giving us the same idea, the same day?!

Lou Ann McClendon—Your dedication and attention to detail amaze me. Thanks for encouraging me to pursue this project and covering me in prayer throughout the process.

Sharon Jaynes—You are a wonderful partner in ministry. Thank you for your many cards of encouragement, your countless prayers on my behalf, and for sharing your many gifts with all of us at Proverbs 31. The world is a better place because of you!

Marie Ogram—You are a gifted woman, and I thank God for bringing you into my life. I could not have done this project without you—many, many thanks!

The Staff at Proverbs 31 Ministries—You amaze and inspire me! Thank you for the privilege of working with such godly people.

The Staff at Renewing the Heart—Thank you for helping make the dream of this book and the leadership conference a reality. You ladies are gracious, gifted, and a whole lot of fun!

Greg, Bill, Elsa, Dave, and the rest of the Moody Press gang—Thank you for once again catching my vision and making it a reality. I know when Jesus thinks of Moody Press, it makes Him smile!

Cheryl Dunlop—Thank you for your sharp eyes and creative suggestions. You are a gifted editor.

Art, Hope, Ashley, and Brooke—Thanks for being the best cheering section a woman could have.

FIRST
THINGS FIRST

My hands were shaking and my voice quivering as I attempted to introduce my guest for the day's radio broadcast. Oh, I was a master at hiding my hurt and fear, but this day was harder than most. Today's guest was the director of a local Crisis Pregnancy Center. My guest had been arranged for me and the scripted questions written by one of our staff members. I walked into the interview totally unprepared for what God was about to do in my heart. You see, for years I'd been carrying secrets, lots of secrets. Secrets about past hurts and mistakes that I thought would destroy my ministry should anyone ever discover the "real" me. So every day, in every public situation, I painted on a big smile, quoted Scriptures as if my heart really believed them, and determined to win the lost and encourage the saints by living the "perfect" life.

After all, isn't that what it's all about . . . acting perfect and encouraging others to do the same? Oh, how mixed up and deceived I was. I faked my way through the interview and couldn't wait to escape to my car. Finally, when I was alone, the tears poured out of my eyes. I kept thinking back to the interview and how the director of the center talked about hope and healing for women. Little did she or any of my staff know that many years ago I'd had an abortion. I desperately wanted what she was talking about, but I was a leader of a ministry, and what would happen if people found out about my horrible secret? I was sure I'd be banned by the whole Christian community and banished from the ministry.

Maybe some of you are in that place right now. As I've traveled around the country speaking, I can't tell you how many pastors' wives, women's ministry directors, and other women's ministry leaders have heard my testimony and afterward come up to me like a deer caught in headlights. Their tear-filled eyes are usually wide with fear as they pull me aside and say, "Me too. I'm living your story."

Though these ladies may have different circumstances surrounding their fear of being real, we have the same common denominator: Satan has been telling us for years that God could never love someone like us and could never really use us, but if we work hard enough at being good and showing others how to be good, then He might have mercy on us. Let me assure you that is a lie straight from the pit of hell. Satan is dogmatic about selling this lie to every

Christian who has ever sinned (which, by the way, is all of us), for he knows if we catch even a glimpse of God's grace and ability to work good from bad, then we would set the world on fire for Christ.

God loves you, my friend. God really loves you . . . not because you're good enough and not because you work hard enough; He loves you just for being you. In His eyes, you are beautiful and wonderful. You are His beloved. Isaiah 54:4 says, "Do not be afraid; you will not suffer shame. Do not fear disgrace; you will not be humiliated. You will forget the shame of your youth." Verse 10 of this same chapter goes on to say, "Though the mountains be shaken and the hills be removed, yet my unfailing love for you will not be shaken."

Do you understand what God is saying here? His love is unconditional, meaning it's not based on what you've done or haven't done. It is based on what He has done. He died on the cross, and His blood now covers your sin. He's calling you to not be afraid any longer and to let go of the shame of your past.

That day in my car after the interview I knew God was calling me to trust Him as I never had before. He wanted me to serve not from the "perfect" platform but from the place of one whose life had been radically redeemed. Slowly, God brought me to a place where I knew I was supposed to tell my testimony to our staff. I was terrified. I was still convinced that in telling my story I would shock our staff so much that they would immediately ask me to step down as their leader. Finally, with tears streaming down my face, I told them my whole story.

Their reaction was not something I could have ever imagined. They gathered around me and poured their love and support on me. Then the miracle happened. God used my story to help them be vulnerable and real. One by one they all told their own stories, some of which were just like mine. God showed me something so amazing that night: I was not alone in my hurt and shame. Every woman has a story. Some are less dramatic than others, but nonetheless we've all fallen short and needed God's grace and forgiveness. We spend our whole lives trying to see if we really measure up, yet the Lord says simply to keep our eyes fixed on Him and to follow Him: "I am the light of the world. Whoever follows me will never walk in darkness, but will have the light of life" (John 8:12).

We need to turn from those dark things that have been holding us captive for so long, listen to His tender mercy, accept His forgiveness, and rejoice in the Light of Life. We need to stop wondering if we really have what it takes to be a leader and realize God doesn't call the qualified; He qualifies the called. He's called you to take part in the Great Commission of telling God's amazing love and freeing truth to others. You are His light in the corner of the world where He has placed you. And make no mistake . . . it is He who put you in just this place, for just this time.

Won't you join me in setting the world on fire for Christ? Oh, what an adventure lies before us as we set forth leading women to the heart of God.

First, let's start with the flame in our own hearts, realizing we can't lead others any farther than we've already journeyed ourselves.

GET A LOVE LIFE—
YOUR OWN INTIMATE
RELATIONSHIP
WITH GOD

Michelle McKinney Hammond

L ove is *definitely* my favorite subject! And I am most certainly not alone. Every talk show examines how to get the love we want. We are constantly reminded from the pulpit that God loves us. But what about *us* loving *God?* Not in the sense that we are all taught to say "I love the Lord," seemingly by rote, but in the sense of cultivating an intimate love relationship with Him. Instead we prefer discussions on how to get God to do what we want. Seven keys to financial freedom. Five tips for stomping on the devil's head (though Christ has already accomplished this, some of us still seem to feel He needs our help) . . . how to this, how to that . . . but rarely do we have full-blown discussions or teaching about being in love with the Lover of our souls. *Why is that?* I've wondered. Perhaps we are all so busy trying to dot our spiritual i's and cross our religious t's that we've forgotten the first and most important reason we are in this thing called Christianity. For relationship. Yes, that's it! We are supposed to be having a *relationship,* a love relationship with our Lord. But why do we spend most of our time concentrating on anything but that?

As I pondered this question, the Lord reminded me of a situation that had occurred in my own life. Several years ago I met a dashing man from France while on Christmas vacation in Ghana, West Africa, where I spent the holidays with my father. He was romantic, passionate, all-consuming, and definitely interested in pursuing a committed relationship with me. We made plans. *Big* plans. He was to finish his course of study in Paris. I was to learn French so that I could converse with his friends when I met them. And we could reconvene in Chicago, where I lived, to continue our life together happily ever after.

Well! Several months after we had both returned to our respective homes, on the heels of a flurry of phone calls and faxes (there wasn't any e-mail at the time), without any prompting I received a "Dear Mary" letter—you know, the feminine equivalent of a "Dear John" letter. The gist of it was, "Dear Michelle, This is difficult for me but I must end our relationship. I find it impossible to continue this from afar, and I love and respect you far too much to lead you on. I feel that the person who is in my life should be close to me, therefore a long distance relationship is not something I wish to pursue. All the best."

Imagine my chagrin! I just didn't understand. After all, I enjoyed the notion of having a boyfriend . . . somewhere! I reveled in the idea of having someone in my life who loved me and longed for me . . . somewhere. I loved having the emotional security of a relationship without the responsibility. Without having to do the maintenance work. Hmmm . . . kinda like how most of us are when it comes to our relationship with God.

LOVE FROM A DISTANCE

We like the idea that we are loved and protected by this awesome, fearsome, all-powerful God who is there for us . . . somewhere. We are happy to know that God knows us and is out there working on our behalf . . . somewhere. The truth of the matter is we love the concept of having a relationship with God, having the benefits of being His daughters and the future bride of Christ, without embracing the responsibility of cultivating the intimacy that is needed to maintain any love covenant.

Why do we do that? What makes us shy away from drawing closer to the heart of God? After all, from the beginning, His first agenda was to be as close to us as He could get. He took the elevator down from heaven to visit Adam and walk and talk with him in the cool of the garden every evening. It was never His intention to have to *write* to us. He longs to *speak* to each of us individually as He did with Abraham, Moses, and many others we read about in the Old Testament (and as Christ spoke to His disciples in the New Testament). But all of that changed because of one disastrous date with the Israelites. After they left Egypt and were on their way through the wilderness, God told Moses He wanted to meet with His people. They set the date, and Moses gave the people instructions to wash themselves, wash their clothes, and abstain from sexual relations for three days. God wanted to meet with a people who were cleansed without and within, with nothing, not even the distractions or residual effect of any other relationship, standing between them.

On that very special day, the Lord came down the mountain and announced the Ten Commandments to the people. They absolutely lost it! They freaked out! They couldn't handle the presence of God. His voice scared them. They told Moses it was too frightening to them. They suggested that he go up, talk to God, and come back down and tell them what God said. Little did they know that they forfeited more than the presence of God that day. They forfeited the up close and personal, intimate fellowship with Him that was needed to solidify their faith for facing the impossible. On that day they crossed the line from relationship to religion. Though their fear was appropriate, their lack of interest in relating to God on any level cost them dearly.

This decision affected far more than just the everyday Joe and Sarah; it affected the leadership as well. Aaron, Nadab, Abihu, and seventy elders were invited to come and meet God after that. They went, saw God, and were not consumed. The Bible says they even sat and ate a meal together in the presence of God, but their actions later would reveal that they were unable to discern the power and glory of God. They had a religious experience that did not change them within. Perhaps they were too busy concentrating on natural bread to really feast from the spiritual bread God had to offer. Aaron went on to build the golden calf for the people to worship when Moses took too long to come back down the mountain, along with those elders. Nadab and Abihu decided to mix up their own concoction for the incense that was to be burned before God, and they were consumed in the fire for offering the wrong type of worship. So much for having an experience with God! He draws so very close, but we are still so far away in our own understanding if we are unwilling to be open to the fullness of Him in our lives.

Could it be fear that keeps us from drawing closer? What is it about God that causes us to head for the hills when He beckons to us? I think Isaiah the prophet summed it up best when telling his experience of seeing God. He said the first thing that occurred to him was his own state of being. "I am a man of unclean lips!" he cried. I think we avoid real intimacy with God because when we see Him as He is, we also see ourselves as we really are, and we look pretty miserable in comparison. It gets even worse. We begin to see everything through His eyes, and the sight is overwhelming when we view the world from God's perspective. Isaiah said in sad realization, "I live among an unclean people" (see

Isaiah 6:5). Seeing things through God's eyes can be quite overwhelming as we realize we are powerless to change the condition of the world as well as ourselves.

Ah, but here is the comfort. God is well aware that we are merely "puffed up dust" as a friend of mine so glibly puts it. He knows we stand in need of His help to become "spiritually correct," and He has made provision for our cleansing through Jesus Christ. Back in Isaiah's day He exhibited this same graciousness by sending a seraph with a hot coal to cleanse Isaiah's lips. As we confess our undoneness, God is faithful to provide the restoration that we need.

But this is only the beginning! Something happens as we enter into right relationship with Him. We are suddenly concerned about what He is concerned about. His burdens and cares become ours. As God pondered whom He could send as a messenger to the nation of Israel, Isaiah, overcome by the presence of God, had the nerve to raise his puny little arm and say, "Here am I. Send me!" How many times in your prayer time have you uttered before God, "Oh Lord, please send someone to do so and so . . ." only to hear the prompting of the Holy Spirit saying, "If that is your burden, then you are the one for the assignment. You see the need; go for it!" *But, Lord, it would be so much more convenient if You sent someone else,* we think. And yet we find ourselves compelled to reach out to a lost and suffering world because we feel God's heart toward His people.

And yet we worry that God is now going to take over our lives. *What else will He require of me? I don't want to be peculiar.* We shudder at the thought. It seems as though when we give God an inch, He takes more than a mile; the path seems unending with its twists and turns. Where will God take me now that I've said yes to Him? What will He do with me now? How many of my own dreams will I have to give up? We, like Isaiah, ask with great trepidation, "How long will I have to keep this up?"

We worry about how others will respond to the changes in our lives.

We, like Moses, who glowed when he came down from his mountain-top experience with God, seek to veil our experiences with God by downplaying His effect on our lives in the presence of others. After all, we don't want to upset anyone or appear too fanatical or religious. And yet we are told to let our light shine before men and women so that God will be glorified. Hmmm, it seems as if it comes down to Him or us, doesn't it? There's not enough room in this temple of flesh for both of us to rule.

GETTING UP CLOSE AND PERSONAL

Why do we need to get past all of these fears and apprehensions to embrace God up close and personal? Because, if we don't, we will never experience the fullness of the blessings and victory we crave for our individual lives, that's why. It is in the secret, intimate place with God that we find our greatest desire is for Him, not the things we struggle to acquire. This is our true reason for existing—fellowship with Him—and all other blessings flow from our peace with Him. If we forfeit the presence of God and interacting with Him on an intimate basis, we lose the greatest key to possessing the faith we need to obtain the desires of our hearts. The Bible tells us that those who know their God will be strong and do exploits! Truly the deeper our relationship, the greater our faith in His abilities to move on our behalf. Our beliefs dictate our actions. Our actions affect our circumstances for better or for worse. Are you getting the connection? It is safe to say that our ability to acquire favor and blessings above and beyond the free gift of salvation have everything to do with how we interact with God.

Now you might say, "You know, Michelle, you are absolutely right! I have allowed my own shame, my own feelings of inadequacy to keep me from drawing closer to God. I have been overwhelmed by all I see around me. I have been afraid of what God would do to me if I made myself available to Him. I've held back because I have not wanted to come out of my comfort zone. Yet I do feel a longing to have a passion for Him. I feel as if I've been merely going through the motions of being a Christian without the joy and the excitement I once had. How do I get it back?"

I hear you. I have been there myself. And God has the answer for us all. In the book of Revelation He advised a church that had grown religious to return to its first love. He acknowledged that its members were good little Christian "do-bees," doing all the right things, but obviously they weren't having a very good time doing it. They were acting out of duty, not love. God wanted them to do the right thing not because they were *supposed* to but because they *wanted* to. Not out of a *subservient* love for Him, but a *passionate* love for Him. He wanted them to be hot for Him. Not lukewarm. He wanted a people who were on fire for Him. If they didn't turn up the heat in their hearts, He threatened to remove their lampstands. Without light they would not be able to see the path that they should take to reflect His light to the world. Without a light they would be of no use. Therefore they would be removed. The light was crucial to their witness, their ability to be a beacon in their community, their effectiveness, their ability to function as a church. In other words, He wasn't "feeling the love," which meant there probably was not a lot of dialogue going on between them. They were no longer seeking His instruction. They were being obedient by rote. They were on automatic, heading toward darkness if they didn't reconnect with Him.

God asked them to remember the height from which they had fallen. To recapture the excitement they felt when they first discovered His love. I think He was saying, "Remember how rich our fellowship was? How you couldn't wait to be in My presence? To talk to Me or to read about Me?" Recall all of that, and repent. That's right. We owe God an apology. Not just to make an admission that we've been remiss in our relationship with Him, but to really acknowledge our laxness from His viewpoint. Consider how you feel when someone you love ignores you or makes you feel as if you are not an important priority. Mm, hmm, I knew you would understand. On that note renew your relationship with God as an old married couple might renew their vows. Refresh your commitment to Him. Start over. Make new plans to be with Him. Find creative ways to spice up your relationship with Him.

It is important to note that when we get to heaven we will not be attending an employee banquet. We will be the collective bride, attending our very own wedding feast. The honeymoon will not be enjoyable if you are not in love with the groom. As a matter of fact, I think it's safe to say if you're not in love with the Groom, you won't be invited! Those trying to sneak into the banquet will be told, "I never knew you." Oh, my sisters, to know Him is to love Him; the two cannot be separated. He is more than wonderful. A faithful Lover of our souls. Altogether lovely and desirable in every way. Why should we love Him so completely? Because He first loved us! He is the embodiment of the perfect love story.

Every woman wants a hero who will pursue her, fight for her, and rescue her from the dragon. Is that a fantasy? No, it is not. They say that truth is stranger than fiction and that fairy tales are birthed from the true desires of our heart. Well, we don't have to stop at the imagery of being swept away by a knight in shining armor when we can have a love affair with the Prince of Peace, the Lord of lords and King of kings, Christ Jesus. Because the true love story is that He left heaven to pursue us. He fought for us by dying on the cross, descending into hell, snatching the keys of hell and death from that dragon Satan, and leading captivity captive. On that note He ascended into heaven, where He is making plans for our wedding day. He is building us a fabulous mansion where we will live and reign with Him forevermore! Now that's a love story I can get into. You can too. After all, the truth of the matter is if you are a part of the body of Christ, not only do you serve Him who is Lord of all, you are engaged to a divine fiancé! You are guaranteed to have a heavenly romance throughout eternity, but God wants it to start right here, right now. So until our ultimate wedding day, all we have to do is keep the fire in our hearts burning with passion and expectancy.

Michelle McKinney Hammond is a speaker and singer at women's conferences, universities, and churches. She is also a cohost of the Emmy-award nominated show *Aspiring Women.* As the Founder and President of HeartWing Ministries she dedicates full-time service to writing and speaking, inspiring Christians to return to the basics of a love-driven relationship with God. She is also the author of more than twelve books including *Get a Love Life: How to Have a Love Affair with God.*

OUT OF THE FISHBOWL
AND INTO THEIR HEARTS

Yvette Maher

The speaker left the stage as the women gathered their things. Based on their reaction, her message to the women at Bible study had clearly been well received. She thanked the Lord for equipping her with peace and the words that would reach the hearts of this hungry group. She put on a big smile and set about meeting and greeting the loyal members of her weekly meetings.

How did she prepare for her talk that day? What was her process for hearing from the Lord? When had she found the quiet time to listen with an obedient ear? How does a public person sort out and do "life" while being seen by eager onlookers? When is she "real"? When does she let her hair down and show her true emotion? Webster defines real as this: "*Existing* in fact, not merely seeming. *Her emotions are real, not imaginary.*"

Have you ever heard someone described with the phrase "She is just so real"? What does that look like? If a well-known personality is being critiqued, her successes may be summed up by observing that she is knowledgeable, outstanding, articulate, or, in some cases, even anointed. The icing on the cake is to observe a speaker after the podium experience as she interacts with people. Perhaps you can catch a glimpse of the person's "realness" at dinner that evening.

Everyone wants the "inside scoop"—what I call the "fishbowl" observation. As a well-known personality, leader in the community, women's ministry director, wife of the pastor, or daughter of a father whose name has just made the headlines, you must accept that people are watching and talking. Some speak with admiration, some with just plain old gossip. Whatever the case may be, *you* are the fish and they are looking to see your "realness."

I think one of the hardest things to understand and live with while serving in leadership, especially in ministry, is the "fishbowl factor." If you can keep the pace going, hair in the latest style, crow's feet lifted, and your events well-attended, you may just survive, or so you think.

If you relate to the scenario of the woman who was teaching the Bible study, when do you let your hair down? When do you release true emotion? What form does your "realness" take? Is it godly? Is it biblically correct to express such emotion? Being real is a foreign concept for many. It requires searching in your heart and asking tough questions that can be answered only by you and the Lord. Again, when are *you* real?

A TRUE LEADER IN THE FISHBOWL

In Genesis, we observe the life of a true leader in a fishbowl—Joseph. As the story goes, his father, Jacob, favors him, setting the scene for serious sibling rivalry. With jealousy setting the scene, the plot finally thickened to include murder. "Here comes that dreamer!" his brothers exclaim. "Come on, let's kill him and throw him into a deep pit. We can tell our father that a wild animal has eaten him. Then we'll see what becomes of his dreams!" His brothers' jealousy over Joseph's position with their father—and his colorful wardrobe—lands this young man in a pit to be claimed by lions, tigers, and bears. Oh my!

What an opportunity to be the victim! Instead, Joseph's example teaches us to be eternal optimists. Make lemonade out of lemons. Thrown into a pit, sold to a band of Ishmaelites, and given up for dead. Talk about hard times! Have you been there? I wonder what the headlines would have said after Joseph became famous and the media began digging through his past to find out the "real" scoop.

As I have become acquainted with women in positions of leadership or influence, it has been amazing to see how their past, or at least their present, is offered up to the public eye—the fishbowl observers. Some openly share their lives with others. With lessons and examples, they display their laundry on public clotheslines. Others appear to be above tragedy or heartbreaking life lessons. I am not the latter. In fact, I make it a deliberate point to share my life openly, because it is too unbelievable not to tell! I couldn't write fiction that is any more captivating than the "real thing." Balance is the key—balance and wisdom.

Joseph didn't map out and plan his future for the position he would someday hold. It was designed for him, and the plans were ordained long before his birth. The Lord knew Joseph's circumstances just as He knows our circumstances. In Joseph's case, he could see that what his brothers meant for evil, the Lord restored for good. Joseph made it a practice to be obedient even when his emotions didn't feel like it. The account of his life is an invaluable lesson in "seeing the glass half-full."

A PRIVATE PLACE OUTSIDE THE FISHBOWL

If you haven't read Joseph's story lately, I encourage you to do it now. (It's found in Genesis 37, 39–50.) Pay particular attention to how he handled the fishbowl experiences. Joseph was a man in charge; he was a leader in high demand, running in very influential circles, handsome and highly favored! All the while, he was also a man burdened with a past and an abundance of pent-up emotion. Can you imagine how he must have yearned for his family's love and acceptance? Surely he had the opportunity to allow "bitter roots" to grow and overtake his garden. He could not openly show his true emotions, and, in most situations, he had to "go away to weep." Notice how many times he wept, where he wept, and the activity that caused him to weep. Beginning with Genesis 42:24 we learn, "he turned away from them and began to weep." The narrative goes on to say that Joseph made a hasty exit because he was overcome with emotion for his brother and wanted to cry. Going into his private room, he wept there (Genesis 43:30).

Do you have a private room where you can weep? My sanctuary is the shower. I have had some of my best crying fits under the running water! Unfortunately, it's not always feasible to stop mid-discussion and proclaim, "I need to take a shower now. Can we continue this conversation later?" As women, we have perfected the "pull-it-together, get-through-the-moment, suck-it-up" facade. Have you ever had a neighbor ring your doorbell at the exact moment that you and your husband are having a "discussion"? You open the door with a big (fake) smile and greet her with, "Oh, come in! We're all fine!" She would never know that mere seconds before you were considering a procedure known as "taking someone's head off in one clean sweep"! The fine art of stuffing it and saving it for later is a technique women have gotten down pat. Joseph knew this trick too. We learn in Genesis 43:31 that after weeping, "he washed his face and came out, *keeping himself under control.* 'Bring on the food!' he ordered." (Sound familiar?) Nothing like a little Ben & Jerry's "Cherry Garcia" to make it all better!

THE NECESSARY BALANCING ACT

Currently, I hold the position of Vice President of Women's Ministries at Focus on the Family. This role allows me incredible opportunities to write, share through devotions, and speak to many groups as a representative of the ministry. On occasion, I participate in Focus's daily radio broadcast, as well as *Renewing the Heart*'s weekly call-in program. While these activities are both exciting and rewarding, it can be frightening and humbling to live in the Focus on the Family "fishbowl."

When to be vulnerable and how much to tell from my life is always a balancing act. How do *you* balance these things? Have you assessed your past and determined that the Lord knows and perhaps has allowed your life's ups and downs not only for your benefit, but also for the good of others?

One story from my own life provides a real window on this point. When Dr. Dobson told me his vision for Women's Ministries in 1998, asking me to consider taking on the responsibilities of vice president over this new division, my shock led me to reply, "Have you prayed about this?" He quickly responded, "Of course I've prayed about this!"

I was shocked, grateful, and humbled that the Lord would use me in this position, because I *know* me. I know my past. I know my inabilities and shortcomings. In my past, I left a trail of consequences as a result of bad choices and selfish desires. I felt the need to tell Dr. Dobson portions of past mistakes to make sure he knew "who" he was asking to be in leadership at the ministry, even knowing that my days of saying yes to the world and all the trappings that accompany what the world delights in ended on August 25, 1990, when I accepted Christ at my ten-year high school reunion. Even though I know what the Lord's grace feels like! Even though I know what forgiveness tastes like!

I know that redemption and freedom from my past are something to experience and live out, not just to speak of as though they are only words on paper. The other shocking point to becoming a vice president was that I do not possess the credentials required for this position. I have never been to college. I have never felt adequate to be in a position of leadership. I have to simply make myself available to Christ and try to walk in obedience and then hold on! The Lord is constantly stretching me outside my comfort zone and into His. With God, all things are possible.

A very dear friend and Christian counselor has helped me understand that a high profile position and "fishbowl" lifestyle require real time with God on a daily basis. We can get so caught up in preparing for Bible study, writing messages for speaking engagements, or keeping the daily tasks going smoothly and without flaw that we neglect the most important element. We need daily quiet time to truly listen to the Savior's leading and instruction in our lives. Another practical lifesaver for me is to journal about my thoughts, prayers, desires, goals, and even frustrations. I have found that writing these things out on paper and rereading my accounts of the Lord's faithfulness makes me more apt to remember the good times—as well as the learning times!

Prayer, quiet time, and spending time with the Lord are all wonderful expressions of our dependency on Him, but there are times in our lives (this side of heaven) when we need to allow an outpouring of emotions in a safe non-fishbowl zone. When are those times for you? Where are they? Do you have a true friend or a few close friends who know you inside and out? I'm not talking about your husband; I'm talking about a true-blue girlfriend. A priceless nugget given to me by my counselor friend was "Get a friend." But run to that friend second, not first. God is first! He will use others in our lives in incredible ways if we will open up and share from the heart. Get real with a godly, wise woman after you've gotten real with the Lord.

You need trusted relationships for those moments when, like Joseph, you know it's time to cut loose and cry it out. Choosing wisely, let your emotions flow. According to Genesis 45:2, Joseph "broke down and wept aloud. His sobs could be heard throughout the palace, and the news was quickly carried to Pharaoh's palace." Paraphrased, it might read this way: "Finally Joseph stopped stuffing and came out from behind his 'leader of the palace' image, allowing his true emotions to be seen and heard by everyone! This was such incredible news that the tabloid media hounds ran with excitement to Pharaoh to let him know just the kind of man who was in charge of his corner of the world. A man with a much different past than expected, a man bigger than his circumstances!" Joseph, the leader, was not afraid or too confined to share his emotions. Whether it was because he had not seen his family or whether he just needed a good cry, he wept. And wept loudly!

When I read this, I gave a resounding, "Hooray for Joseph!" Hooray for me! No more hiding in the shower to cry! I am free to cry when and where I need to release my emotions—even out in public in the realness of whatever situation might occur. So what if the person behind the podium isn't perfect? There is only One who is perfect—only He who came to "set us free." Amen and amen to the many people in Scripture who allowed their imperfections to make them willing vessels for God's use and glory. This realization shows me that I can be counted among those used by God in spite of who we are. Being real is a scary place to be, unless and until our authenticity is received with love and acknowledged as God's sweetest expression of grace. Learning to foster an air of grace with those we minister with and to is the secret of getting out of the fishbowl and into their hearts.

Yvette Maher is the Vice President of Renewing the Heart Women's Ministries at Focus on the Family. Previously, Yvette served as Director of the Constituent Response department, Focus's first point of contact for all mail and phone calls received by the ministry. Her experience in that position has given her valuable insight and a heightened sensitivity to the many challenges people face in today's society, while her current role gives her the opportunity to focus her attention specifically on the needs of women.

THREE

HOW GOD EQUIPS
US FOR MINISTRY

Lysa TerKeurst

I remember the day I caught my first glimpse of what my mission in life would be. I was sitting in my den with tears streaming down my cheeks staining the pages of the Bible study book I held in my hand. The question I was trying to answer for that week's lesson dealt with whether or not I would do whatever God asked of me. At first my answer was, of course, whatever God wants me to do, I'll do.

As I attempted to go on to the next question, I felt God speaking to my heart, "Will you tell your testimony?" In a panic I closed the book and started praying out loud. I told God I would do anything except tell the painful experiences from my past. A picture popped into my head of all the people who would reject me if they knew the secrets of my past. No way, not in a million years, would I ever be able to give my testimony. Besides, how could God use my junk for His glory?

I felt God again speak to my heart, "What the devil meant for evil, I will use for good. Trust Me, Lysa, trust Me." I knew I was at a major crossroads in my spiritual journey. God was pointing in one direction, and I was running in the opposite direction. I had to decide whether or not I was going to obey God. By the end of our time together I reluctantly told God that at my next speaking engagement I would tell part of my testimony. A few weeks later I stood before a group of women and did just that. Tear-stained faces all over the room confirmed that this was a message women needed to hear. God used the story of a broken vessel to pour out His love, comfort, and compassion. Several women were saved, and more than half recommitted their lives to Christ. I witnessed a miracle of God that day, and I have never been the same.

As I drove home that evening, I told God that I would go to the ends of the earth and tell everything about my life with whoever would listen. I have traveled all over the U.S., and God has been faithful to His promises. What the devil meant for evil, God truly has used for His glory. This is the mission God has for me in my role as a servant of Christ. I am to be a transparent person who allows God to take the pain of my past and use it as a bridge that others may walk from darkness into His wonderful healing light.

I want women to know that God desires to use them as well. You see, we each have a story. Things have happened in our lives in such a way that only God could comfort us. We are responsible to pass on God's comfort to others. Remember—God doesn't comfort us to make us comfortable, He comforts us to make us comfort-*able*: able to be used as vessels through which God can pour out His mercy, love, and comfort to others. Let me ask you the question that changed my life: *Are you willing to do whatever God asks of you?*

I love the story about a little boy and his grandfather walking along the beach after a storm. Hundreds of starfish had washed up on the shore, and the little boy was busy picking them up and throwing them back into the water. The grandfather asked the little boy why he was doing this, because he could not possibly save them all. The little boy looked at the starfish in his hand and replied, "No, but I can save this one." You'll never know what kind of difference you can make until you surrender your desires for your life to the perfect mission of God.

THE NECESSARY EQUIPMENT

In order to get a clear vision of your mission, you must understand three important biblical truths. You are a new *creation* of God, who has been *chosen* by God to fulfill a *calling* from God. God has uniquely equipped you to answer the calling of your mission. You have been given experiences, qualifications, unique spiritual gifts, interests, and a certain personality type. Notice that when you take the first letter of each of these words, they spell EQUIP.

Experiences

Have you ever asked God, "God, why did You let this happen to me?" I have asked this question so many times. I have asked it in times of sorrow as well as in times when I have made a complete fool of myself. My life has been such a comedy of errors at times. I now know that God gave me all these things so that I could empathize with those in pain and tell funny stories, letting people know how very human I am. God has given you experiences to use for His glory as well. The wonderful thing for Christians is that God promises us that He will work all things together for the good of those who love Him. James 1:2–4 says, "Consider it pure joy, my brothers, whenever you face trials of many kinds, because you know that the testing of your faith develops perseverance. Perseverance must finish its work so that you may be mature and complete, not lacking anything."

Imagine sitting down at a table with two cups of flour, three eggs, a teaspoon of vanilla, one cup of sugar, a half teaspoon of baking powder, and a few other ingredients. You taste the sugar and it is good, but when you taste the baking powder it is bitter. You continue to taste the ingredients, some tasty and some downright gross. This is like life. Some of the events in your life are sweet like the sugar, others dry like the flour, and still others that you don't like at all. However, using Jesus' perfect recipe, all of the events in your life will be mixed together and put through some intense heat—and then you will rise. Just as a cake would not be the same if you left out some of the ingredients, so Jesus wants to use all of your experiences to make you complete and able to be used for His glory.

Qualifications

Your qualifications are your skills and abilities, those things that you do well either through training and education or natural ability. Exodus 31:3 gives us the example of God telling Moses that He has given a person skills, abilities, and knowledge in all kinds of crafts.

Now before you say that you have no skills or abilities, let me assure you that the average person possesses around six hundred skills and abilities, according to Rick Warren in his "Purpose Driven Church" seminar. The key is to match your abilities with a place of ministry. For example, some of Jesus' disciples were fishermen. They could use what they were already good at in a place of ministry. Not that they would actually haul in loads of people with nets, but rather that they knew how to cast nets that would attract. So instead of fishing nets, they cast out the Word of God into the hearts of people.

An example from my life is the ability to write poems. This is something I use to express, through rhyming words, pictures of life that touch people's hearts. My friend Glynnis has the ability to edit. Whereas she used to use this skill in the workplace, she now uses it in ministry by editing the newsletter of Proverbs 31 Ministries, "The P31 Woman."

Another friend of mine, Lynn, has the ability to decorate for events in such a way that makes people feel welcome and special. There are many different abilities from accounting to public relations to teaching aerobics. Take time to start a list of your abilities that might be used in some way to glorify God.

Unique Spiritual Gifts

These are gifts, *your* gifts. Remember—these gifts are given to us in seed form. We must cultivate and use these gifts to see them develop. One of my gifts is evangelism. I love to share the gospel with people, and God gives me the most wonderful opportunities to do so.

Several years ago we had a second phone line installed in our home that was only one digit off from the long distance information line in a region of South Carolina. At first I was so frustrated with the influx of callers wanting phone numbers to Bud's Seafood and Bessie's Best Bathing Suit Shop. Just as I was about to call the phone company and demand they fix the problem immediately, God reminded me of my commitment to make the most of every opportunity He gives me.

So the "God line" was born. I started proudly answering the phone, "God-line information. We don't have all the answers, but we know the One who does. How may I help you?" Most of the time I get a bewildered "Huh?" on the other end, but every now and then God uses this wrong number to set divine appointments with Him. (By the way, my other home number is only one digit off from the local pizza parlor. God has such a sense of humor!) Let me encourage you to look for ways to cultivate your gifts. I can promise you will see them grow and flourish.

Interests

You have two types of interests: intense interests and fun interests. Intense interests are topics or issues that you feel passionate about. If

45

you were given an opportunity to address the world for one hour on prime-time television, what would you talk about? If I had this chance, I would tell my testimony about abortion—not to condemn those who have had one but rather to offer them the hope and healing that I have found through Jesus. I would also encourage anyone who is considering an abortion to have an ultrasound and see for herself the tiny heart that beats within the little unborn child. I would tell women and girls that although this child may seem like a mistake to them, it is not a mistake to God. God has great plans for this baby. He will bring people to help pregnant girls who feel alone and afraid. This is my intense interest.

Your interests also consist of things you consider fun. If you had an entire day to do anything, what would you do? Well, for me I'd go snow-skiing with friends and family. Don't ask me how, as a native Floridian, I acquired such a passion for hitting the slopes. It just happened. I'm hooked. This is one of my fun interests and what I'd do if given a free day.

Personality

This is the way you express yourself and relate to other people. Some of us are introverts, whereas others of us are extroverts. Some of us are task oriented; others are people oriented. You have been given a personality perfectly suited for what God intends for you to do. I am an extroverted, people-oriented person. I love to have fun—so let's play a quick game. Put this book down for just a minute and get your lipstick tube. Do you have it in hand? (If you're like me, you ran to get your lipstick and got sidetracked somewhere between your purse and the junk drawer in your kitchen. It has probably taken you several hours to make your way back to this book. If you're one of those task-oriented people, you've probably skipped this game and are sticking to the task of reading the rest of this chapter.) OK, pull out your tube and examine its shape. According to a very "official" lipstick personality chart given to me at a church retreat, you might discover that your lipstick really can tell a lot about you.

> *Group one:* Flat-top lipstick people
>> To the point, high morals, conservative, very dependable
> *Group two:* Rounded, smooth-tip lipstick people
>> Easy-going, peacemaker, steady, generous
> *Group three:* Sharp-angled-tip lipstick people
>> Opinionated, high-spirited, outgoing, likes attention
> *Group four:* Sharp-angled but curved-tip lipstick people
>> Creative, enthusiastic, energetic, talkative, loves attention, falls in love easily, needs a schedule but dislikes one
> *Group five:* Sharp angles on both sides lipstick people
>> Curious, mysterious, faithful, looks for the easy way, loves life
> *Group six:* Original slant- and tip-shape lipstick people
>> Abides by the rules, great follower, does not like too much attention, somewhat reserved, likes a schedule

Remember, no matter what shape your lipstick or what kind of personality you have, the key is to discover your personality's attributes and make the most of those while seeking to improve on your personality's weaknesses.

This special EQUIPment is for you to use to help you fulfill God's calling in each role you play. For each stage of your life, you will be required to play different roles. As you choose the roles you will play, you need to limit your commitment in roles that are less significant.

USING YOUR EQUIPMENT
IN LIFE'S MAJOR ROLES

You should focus your energy on making the most of your major roles. You can apply the 80/20 rule. You then dedicate 80 percent of your time to your major roles and 20 percent of your time to other less significant roles. After you decide what your major roles are, pull out your calendar and see if your schedule matches your calling.

When I did this I found a source of great frustration in my life. I was wasting significant time on insignificant things. For example, my calendar was filled with meetings for things that were not part of my calling. I finally realized that life would not stop if I pulled out of some of those activities. You see, too many of us are too busy to find our mission in life. We are consumed with participating in everything, and as a result we are not effectively making a difference in anything.

Others are at the opposite extreme of this and are not doing anything. Either out of feelings of inadequacy or laziness, they simply sit on the sidelines of life and watch as others pass by. Both of these are tragic situations. Life should not be something that just "happens" to you; it should be something that you live to the very fullest, determined to do all that God created you to do.

In the parable of the talents found in Matthew 25:14–30, Jesus told of a master who entrusted three servants with a certain number of talents. One servant, who was given five talents, decided to invest his talents and earned the master's praise and respect. Because the servant had been faithful with a few talents, he was given more. The servant who was given two talents also earned his master's praise and respect for investing wisely and getting a return on his investment. However, the third servant was called wicked and lazy for burying the one talent he had been given and not doing anything productive with it. His talent was taken from him, and he was cast out into darkness. Which servant can you identify with?

God has entrusted us with much. He has given us life, and He wants to see that we are investing our lives wisely. I don't know about you, but I want to make my Master proud. I long to hear, "Well done, My good and faithful servant." To those who give good accounts and live their lives wisely, God will affirm their efforts with encouragement, and He will entrust more to them. Do you want to live an abundant and fulfilling life? Invest your talents wisely. Use what God has given you to fulfill your purpose and answer the call of your mission.[1]

Lysa TerKeurst is a wife, mother of three daughters, and President of Proverbs 31 Ministries. She has been featured on *The 700 Club, Focus on the Family, How to Manage Your Money* with Larry Burkett, and Billy Graham's *Decision Today* radio program. Lysa is one of the voices behind the Proverbs 31 radio program heard daily from coast to coast. She has also written *Seven Life Principles for Every Woman, Who Holds the Key to Your Heart?, Living Life on Purpose, Capture Her Heart* (for husbands), and *Capture His Heart* (for wives). Lysa is also an inspirational speaker for women's events and marriage conferences throughout the country.

---

[1] This chapter is a slight revision from Lysa TerKeurst's book *Living Life on Purpose* (Chicago: Moody, 2000), 49–56.

BUILDING YOUR CONFIDENCE TO LEAD AND TEACH

Sharon Jaynes

I hope the mere fact that this chapter is included in *Leading Women to the Heart of God* gives you some reassurance. Most women who feel called to minister to others feel somewhat inadequate for the task and insecure in taking on the role of "leader." If someone is totally confident in her own abilities, I daresay she may not be the person for the job.

I can still remember the panic I felt when God called me to work in a leadership role in Proverbs 31 Ministries. "Lord," I complained, "You know I don't like speaking in front of people. I can't run an international ministry. Why, I'm just a homemaker." After I reminded God of several of my other shortcomings, He took me on a spiritual treasure hunt to discover the type of men and women He chooses to carry out His plans.

GOD'S CHOSEN LEADERS

Moses was one of history's great leaders. After being raised in Pharaoh's household as his grandson, he reached forty years of age and decided that he was ready to save the Israelite nation from slavery. He devised a plan—which failed miserably. Then Moses ran away and took care of sheep in the desert for the next forty years. He was so insecure that he developed a speech impediment and preferred the company of smelly sheep to people. It was then, at Moses' lowest point in life, that God decided he was ready for leadership. God appeared to Moses in a burning bush and called him to lead the Israelite nation out of Egypt.

Moses argued fervently with God. "You've got the wrong person! I can't even speak without stuttering. Have you considered my brother, Aaron?" Four times Moses said, "What if this happens, what if this happens, what if this happens . . ." And each time God answered, "I will do it for you."

That is the same answer God gives us today. See, when Moses thought he was ready at age forty, he wasn't. When he thought he wasn't ready at age eighty, he was. When are we ready to do the impossible for God? We are ready when He calls us and when we know that we cannot do anything in our own strength but only by the power of God working in us. Once Moses believed God would do the leading, he had the confidence to move forward.

Gideon is another mighty warrior who argued with God's choice of leadership. When God chose Gideon to become the leader of the Israelite army, the future leader was busy in a winepress threshing wheat. Now, ladies, you don't usually thresh wheat in a winepress. You thresh wheat by throwing it up in the air in an open field and letting the wind blow away the chaff while the grain falls to the ground. So what was he doing in the winepress? Gideon was so terrified of his enemies he was hiding. And yet, when the angel of the Lord came to him, he addressed Gideon as "O valiant warrior"! (Judges 6:12 NASB). Can't you just see Gideon looking around and saying, "You talking to me?"

Yes, God called him "valiant warrior" because He knew what Gideon could be if he trusted in God's power to work through him.

Then there's one of the most powerful leaders of all time—King David. When the prophet Samuel went to Jesse's house to anoint the next king of Israel, he asked to see each of Jesse's sons. One by one the strapping young men paraded before Samuel for inspection, but God rejected them all. Confused, Samuel asked Jesse, "Is that it? Do you have any more sons?"

Jesse thought a moment and replied, "Oh, I forgot. I do have one more son. Little David is out in the field taking care of the sheep." David was so insignificant to his family that his father had forgotten all about him.

When Samuel saw this young lad, and God gave him the thumbs up, even he doubted God's choice. Samuel thought David's tall, dark, and handsome brother Eliab looked much more like king material than little David. But God answered Samuel's objections when He refused Eliab, "Do not consider his appearance or his height, for . . . man looks at the outward appearance, but the LORD looks at the heart" (1 Samuel 16:7).

What about the women in the Bible? If you were God and were going to list only four women in the lineage of Jesus, whom would you choose? I'd perhaps select Mrs. Noah, Mrs. Moses, or the lovely Mrs. Abraham. But God had a different idea. In Matthew 1, He listed Tamar, who had an incestuous encounter with her father-in-law; Rahab, who had been a prostitute; Ruth, who was a foreigner from a cursed land; and Bathsheba, who had an affair with King David. These are perhaps not whom we would choose, but it is a wonderful example of 1 Corinthians 1:26–31, which says that God deliberately seeks out the weak things and the despised things because it is from them that He can receive the greatest glory.

GOD'S WORK WITHIN HIS CHOSEN LEADERS

Do you feel weak, ordinary, and even a bit fearful? Well, congratulations! You are exactly who God is looking for to lead His people and bring glory to His name.

I remember when Anne Graham Lotz, Billy Graham's daughter, first began her ministry. She was taken to a soccer stadium in Southern India that was filled with thousands of expectant people and asked to give an evangelistic message like her daddy. Although Anne told her hosts that she was not a preacher, she stepped into the pulpit and preached. She said, "I was sitting there thinking, 'I'm an American housewife. I don't belong here.' But I stepped aside and let God take over. And it's amazing what He can do."[1]

Once we do take those first steps of obedience, it is crucial to remember that it is God who will bring the results. I love the account of Charles Spurgeon's most "ghastly" sermon as it was told in *The Prayer of Jabez Devotional.*

In late nineteenth-century England, Charles Spurgeon was by all accounts the greatest preacher in the capital of the most powerful nation on earth. Huge throngs, including the wealthy and powerful, came to London's cavernous Metropolitan Tabernacle to hear him preach the gospel.

Spurgeon held himself to towering standards, always fearing his best wasn't good enough. One day, his worst fears were realized when he preached an awful sermon. He was so traumatized by his poor work that he rushed home and fell to his knees. "O Lord, I'm so feeble and You're so powerful!" he prayed. "Only You can make something of such a ghastly sermon. Please use it and bless it."

You or I might have told him to put his failure behind him and move on, but Spurgeon kept praying all week for God to use this terrible sermon. Meanwhile, he set about to do better the following Sunday.

And he did. At the conclusion of that sermon, the audience of thousands all but carried him out on their shoulders.

But Spurgeon was not to be fooled. He decided to keep careful records of the result of the two sermons. Within a few months the outcome was clear. The "ghastly" sermon had led forty-one people to know Christ; his masterpiece had led to no observable results at all.

Spurgeon knew or suspected what most forget: Our success in ministry is never about ability in the first place, but about God's power and our dependence on it. Spurgeon leaned on God in his weakness, and God blessed his flawed efforts.[2]

As you begin your journey in leading women to the heart of God, always remember that it is God who is at work in you. Nothing takes the place of preparation. God does not bless laziness. But the results are in His hands. That should give you great confidence.

Let me tell you about my own personal struggle in saying "yes" to the Lord calling me to leadership. I had been praying for God to show me how He wanted me to minister to women for about a year when I met Lysa TerKeurst. She invited me to be a guest on the Proverbs 31 Ministries radio program to speak on infertility. After the recording session, Lysa asked me to be her partner in ministry.

Amazingly, we had been praying for the same number of months. God took two people who had a need and brought them together to meet the needs of women all around the globe. Why didn't He answer our prayers the first month we prayed? I believe it is because He was preparing us, molding us, and maturing us.

Now I have to tell you, I argued with the Lord just like Moses. "God, You've got to be kidding. My voice is too Southern to do radio!" Then I thought about my friends Billy Graham and Charles Stanley. (I hadn't met Beth Moore yet.) "Well, Lord, my college degree is in dental hygiene, not public speaking!" Then I remembered His words to Moses, "I, even I, will be with your mouth, and teach you what you are to say"

(Exodus 4:12 NASB). "But God, I don't know anything about radio!" Then He reminded me of Bezalel and Oholiab, whom He put in charge of working with gold and silver for the tabernacle. These guys had been making bricks with mud and straw as slaves for the Egyptians their entire lives, but God filled them with wisdom, understanding, and knowledge to do the task He called them to do (Exodus 31:1–6).

So I agreed to at least pray about it. What happened next is recorded in *Seven Life Principles for Every Woman.* That summer my husband and I went to Bermuda for a romantic vacation. On one particular evening, Steve and I went on a dining adventure to a five-star restaurant filled with men and women dressed in their very finest evening apparel. In one corner of the dining area, a four-man instrument ensemble filled the room with fluid sounds of music from the 1940s and 1950s. At one point, Steve urged, "Come on, Sharon. Let's go take a spin on the dance floor."

"No way," I replied. "Nobody else is out there. I'm not going to be the only one out there with everyone staring at me. And suppose we mess up. I'd be embarrassed. It's been a long time since we've danced, and I don't remember all the steps. Let's wait until there are some other people dancing. Then I'll go."

Finally the first couple approached the floor. They looked like professional dancers, moving as one and never missing a beat. This did not encourage me at all, but only strengthened my resolve that this was no place for my feet to tread. Then a second couple whose steps weren't quite as perfect joined the first. Reluctantly I agreed to go to a hidden spot on the floor where no one could see us.

After a few minutes, I noticed a fourth couple approach the floor. The man of this couple was in a wheelchair. He was slightly balding with a neatly trimmed beard. On his left hand he wore a white glove, I guessed to cover a skin disease. As the band played a peppy beat, the wife held her love's healthy right hand and danced with him. He spun her around as she stooped to conform to his seated position. Lovingly, like a little fairy child, she danced around his chair, and when the orchestra slowed to a lazy romantic melody, she pulled a chair up beside her beloved and they held each other in a dancer's embrace.

My heart was so moved by this love story unfolding before my eyes that I had to turn my head and bury my face on Steve's shoulder so no one would see the tears streaming down my cheeks. As I did, I saw this rigid, formal dining room was filled with men and women with tears trickling down their cheeks.

After watching this incredible display of love and courage, I realized that my inhibitions of not wanting others to watch me because my steps were not perfect were gone. The Lord spoke to my heart in a powerful way. "Sharon, I want you to notice, who moved this crowd to tears? Was it couple number one, with their perfect steps? Or was it the last couple who not only did not have perfect steps, but one partner had no steps at all? No, My child, it was the display of love, not perfection, that had an effect on the people watching."

See, the Lord doesn't expect our steps to be perfect. He just expects us to be obedient, to take the first step, and to let Him do the rest. The man in the wheelchair never even moved his feet, but his wife did the moves for him. And we need to remember that the Lord will do it for us. We also need to remember that it is not perfect steps that the world is so desperately longing for. The world isn't impressed by supposedly perfect people who live in perfect houses with perfect children. People are impressed by love—genuine God-inspired love. That's what moves a crowd. That should give us great confidence.[3]

I am excited to see how God is going to use you to build His kingdom. Take courage, my friend: God is able to do exceedingly abundantly more than we could ask or think. How amazing that He chooses to do it through us.

Sharon Jaynes is Vice President of Proverbs 31 Ministries, Inc., and co-host for the ministry's international radio segments. She is a feature writer for the Proverbs 31 monthly newsletter, author of many books, including *Being a Great Mom, Raising Great Kids; Seven Life Principles for Every Woman;* and *Celebrating a Christ-Centered Christmas,* and an inspirational speaker for women's events from coast to coast.

1 Gustav Niebuhr and Laurie Goodstein, "Who Will Be the Next Billy Graham?" *The Charlotte Observer,* 2 January 1999, 15A.

2 Bruce Wilkinson, *Prayer of Jabez Devotional* (Sisters, Oreg.: Multnomah, 2001), 62–63.

3 Sharon Jaynes and Lysa TerKeurst, *Seven Life Principles for Every Woman: Refreshing Ways to Prioritize Your Life* (Chicago: Moody, 2001), 237–38.

F I V E

KEEP THE HOME FIRES BURNING—FINDING BALANCE BETWEEN MINISTRY AND FAMILY

Lysa TerKeurst

Just in case you thought you were going to hear from someone in this chapter who always strikes a perfect balance in all areas of her life, let me admit a few things right up front.

Sometimes I stink at being a mom. I know it's been a bad day when my bedtime prayers with the kids go something like this: "Jesus, please help us all to be nicer tomorrow. And please help the kids stay in their bed so Mommy doesn't go crazy!"

I also sometimes stink at being a wife. Especially when I have the "Princess Must Scream" disorder . . . (PMS). Oh, how dramatic I can be as I say those famous last words, "No one appreciates me around here!"

And then there's the diet thing. I stink at that too! I just love standing in the grocery store line with a bag of chips in one hand and a gallon of ice cream in the other hand while skinny air-brushed models stare at me from the magazine rack. I look down at my tummy that's gotten a little rounder with each child and my thighs that now clap for me as I walk.

Oh, and let's don't even venture to the fashion thing. Let's just say that my friends have banned me from wearing white shoes in the dead of winter.

I don't know if you can relate to all my shortcomings, but I bet most of you can identify with at least one. I am convinced that most women struggle at times with feeling that they just don't measure up.

MEASURING UP

A few months ago, I was in the bathroom bathing my youngest daughter when my middle child ran into the bathroom, threw down a measuring stick, and pulled a black string that she had attached to the stick all the way up to the middle of her little six-year-old forehead. She smiled and proudly announced that she'd thought of a new rule for our household. Whenever someone came over to our house, if the person were as tall as the string she'd get a piece of candy. Well, I knew where this was coming from. Just a few days earlier we'd been at an amusement park where Ashley discovered that she was too short to ride many of the rides her older sister was enjoying. She'd been broken-hearted at not "measuring up" to their height requirements.

I smiled at Ashley and told her I liked her rule, but I wanted to add something to it. Whoever is as tall as the string gets *a* piece of candy, but whoever is shorter than the string gets *two* pieces of candy. She looked a little confused and disappointed. I cupped her sweet face in my hands and said, "How tall a person stands is not determined by their height but rather their heart. Ashley, you have a very big heart; therefore you stand very tall in my eyes and more importantly in God's eyes."

At that she smiled, turned, and happily skipped out of the bathroom, leaving her measuring stick behind.

That's when it hit me. The very words I had just spoken to my child were words God had been trying to say to me. God doesn't measure my worth by how skinny my thighs are, or what kinds of clothes I wear, or even by my failures and successes in the wife and mother arena.

That's a message we all need to hear. We must turn from those things that have been making us feel so inadequate and insecure and feel Him cup our face in His loving hands, listen to His tender mercy, accept His definition of our incredible worth, and leave our measuring stick behind. We all mess up at times. We all sometimes stink in our roles as mothers and wives. We all have gotten caught up in a rage of hormones and said things we wish we would not have said to our dear families. And I don't know a woman alive who is completely happy with her body. The white shoe thing is most likely a problem unique to me, but nonetheless God loves me. And He loves you too, my friend.

In God's eyes we do measure up as long as we remember to look up. God will give us just enough patience and love for being great moms today, but we must ask Him. God will give us just enough grace and respect for our husbands today, but we must ask Him. God will give us just enough confidence for today to accept ourselves as the beautiful creatures God made us to be, but we must ask Him.

Do you remember in Exodus the story of God's providing the Israelites with just enough manna for each day? If they took more than a day's supply and tried to store it up, it would spoil. The only exception was that God allowed them to collect two days' worth the day before the Sabbath. Why wouldn't God allow them to store up a whole week's worth or even a whole month's worth at a time? I believe it is because God wanted them to come to Him every day to receive their portion. He wanted their daily dependence. He wants this same thing from us.

When I wake up in the morning and dedicate myself and all the many roles I play to God and ask Him to fill me, I am a good mom and a good wife. I start the day simply saying, "God, today I choose You. I choose Your truth over Satan's lies. I choose to exemplify the fruit of Your Spirit in me . . . love, joy, peace, and patience today. Create in me a clean heart, one that pleases You by all I say and do. Order my steps, Lord. You set this day's agenda for me. Help me to accept myself as Your beloved child, an heir of Your throne, beautiful in Your sight. Oh yeah, and God, if You could make it OK to wear white shoes in heaven anytime of the year, that would really be great, too!"

Proverbs 3:5–6 says, "Trust in the LORD with all your heart and lean not on your own understanding; in all your ways acknowledge him, and he will make your paths straight."

BALANCING MINISTRY AND FAMILY

Balancing the demands of ministry and family can be tough. But I know firsthand how dedicating my day to God first makes all the difference. Here are some other things that have helped me to keep the home fires burning strong.

Have a Meeting of the Minds with Your Husband

For years I placed unrealistic expectations on myself because I thought I knew what I needed to do to be a great wife to my husband. I ran myself ragged trying to keep up "the perfect wife charade." Then one day the thought occurred to me that I had never stopped to ask my husband his definition of a good wife. His answer was simple: "Take good care of the kids, exercise to stay in shape, and keep the house tidy."

I was stunned and wondered, *That's it? Where are the 500 other things I thought I needed to be doing for you that have resided on my to-do list all these years?*

He helped me to see that if I did these top three things he felt very happy and well taken care of. The other things that needed to be done could be delegated to another family member, and he was the first to volunteer. He now does all the grocery shopping and is happy to do it.

All it took was a simple question. Try asking your husband his definition of a good wife—you might be surprised and relieved by his answer!

Get Intentional with a Schedule

I keep a pretty busy speaking schedule that requires me to travel out of town. People often ask me how Art and I make this work with three children. The answer is quite simple: We are intentional with my schedule. Every year before I start booking engagements for the next year, I ask Art to walk through the calendar with me and determine how much I can book and when. Once I have his blessing on my schedule, I am free to book events that fit within the guidelines we've agreed upon.

This same principle can work with any type of scheduling, from weekly Bible studies or participating on committees to girls' nights out. The key is respecting your husband and communicating in advance how you will need him to help you.

Stay Tuned In to Your Children

Every night at dinner we ask the kids to tell their high and their low from that day. This fosters a priceless air of openness in our family conversations. I know that it is my responsibility to make my home the place where my children get the three things that their hearts long for: love, acceptance, and honor. If my children find these needs met within the safety of our home, they won't go looking elsewhere.

My daughters long to know that they are loved for who they are, accepted just as they are, and honored as priceless blessings from God. They are my greatest mission field—my most treasured ministry. I know a threat to doing my best as a mom is busyness. My ministry is wonderfully fulfilling, and in many ways it has made me a better mom, but I know that I have to keep first things first and that my schedule should not crowd out my priority blessings.

Realize That Sometimes the Best Answer Is No

There will be times when ministry opportunities come our way that conflict with our responsibilities to our families. This is the time to delegate to someone else, postpone the ministry opportunity to a later time, or graciously decline. I've had to learn the hard way that it is better to say no right up front when I know an activity or event will stretch me too thin than to agree to participate and make my family suffer.

I pray these simple insights will help you keep those home fires burning. Oh, and if you ever have those days like me when you fall flat on your face, I pray you know whose face to seek. He'll brush you off, wipe your tears, and remind you that you do measure up! In His eyes, you stand very tall.

Lysa TerKeurst is a wife, mother of three daughters, and President of Proverbs 31 Ministries. She has been featured on *The 700 Club, Focus on the Family, How to Manage Your Money* with Larry Burkett, and Billy Graham's *Decision Today* radio program. Lysa is one of the voices behind the Proverbs 31 radio program heard daily from coast to coast. She has also written *Seven Life Principles for Every Woman, Who Holds the Key to Your Heart?, Living Life on Purpose, Capture Her Heart* (for husbands), and *Capture His Heart* (for wives). Lysa is also an inspirational speaker for women's events and marriage conferences throughout the country.

PART TWO

STARTING A
WOMEN'S MINISTRY

Why are we doing all of this in the first place? That's the question we all should be asking, whether we are just starting a women's ministry or running a well-established one that has been around for years. When it all boils down, why are we doing what we are doing? Is it to fill our time and the time of those on our committees? Is it because that's just the way things have always been done? Is it because other churches seem successful in doing things this way? Or is it because God has laid it on our hearts to lead women to Him and we are being obedient to His call?

Andrew Murray, in his book *The Secret of Spiritual Strength*, said,

> The question is often asked, What is the reason for the weak spiritual lives of so many Christians? This is an excellent question, for it is remarkable how little

the church responds to Christ's call, how little it is what Christ wants her to be. What really is the matter? What actually is needed? Various answers may be given, but there is one answer that includes them all: each believer needs the full revelation of a personal Christ as an indwelling Lord, as a satisfying portion.[1]

That's what women inside and outside the church are desperate to find—a real revelation of who Jesus is and what this means to them personally. How is Jesus going to make a difference in helping a woman manage her emotions, make a difference in her marriage, become a better mother, and learn to be a better friend? Jesus can and will help us in all areas of our lives, but there's more. Jesus wants to be our satisfying portion and fill the deep longings in our hearts for which the world has no answer.

We have the answer. That's why we are doing all of this. As we venture into the chapters of this section, let's not lose sight of this. It's all about leading women to the heart of God.

---

[1] Andrew Murray, *The Secret of Spiritual Strength* (rept., New Kingston, Pa.: Whitaker House, 1997), 22.

SIX

IT ALL STARTS WITH PRAYER

Mary Ann Ruff

Every ministry has a birthday, but how do you measure just where the life of a work of God begins? I want to tell you the story of one local church's women's ministry that was conceived in the heart of God, given shape and form in the hearts of women, fleshed out in acts of service, maintained in vitality, and finally measured—all at the place of prayer.

MINISTRY CONCEIVED IN PRAYER

In 1992 my husband was invited to serve as associate pastor of Forest Hill Presbyterian Church in Charlotte, North Carolina. Moving to Charlotte from Kansas City would mean leaving my extended family and a church we had loved and served for seventeen years. When we arrived in Charlotte, I was sure of my husband's calling, but what was mine? I began to earnestly seek God at the place of prayer.

In 1996 David Chadwick, our senior pastor, approached me about overseeing the church's women's ministry on a part-time basis. He appointed a task force of women representing each stage of life to determine a vision for women's ministry at Forest Hill. If I felt called by God to the vision the women identified, then I would accept the position. David asked church member Mary Lance Sisk to chair the task force of eight women. Mary Lance was well known in the church and community—indeed, around the world—as a woman of uncommon prayer, and she eagerly agreed to help.

Believing that the foundation of any work for the kingdom of the Lord Jesus Christ must be prayer, Mary Lance began, ended, and bathed every meeting in prayer. She held the absolute certainty that if we sought the Lord Jesus, we would hear His voice and know how to proceed.

"As we sought God, what He impressed upon our hearts was the Great Commandment—to love God and to love our neighbor," recalls Mary Lance. "Women are weary of 'church programs.' We sensed that the Lord was telling us to get outside the four walls of the church and to reach out to the women He had placed all around us—particularly in the neighborhoods in which we live and work." We had our answer. The women's ministry at Forest Hill would be organized around the twin goals of prayer and evangelism. We were being called by God to go into our community to lead women to the heart of God.

As the goals of the women's ministry resonated in my heart, the Lord confirmed His call to me to lead the effort. The session, our church's governing body, gave enthusiastic approval to our proposed vision and mission for the women's ministry. Now, it was time to seek God afresh for His plan to make the vision a reality.

MINISTRY GIVEN SHAPE
AND FORM IN PRAYER

Since we were called to prayer first, that seemed the best place to start . . . again. The Lord was faithful to engrave two specific prayers upon my heart. I began to earnestly ask according to 2 Chronicles 16:9 . . . that His eyes would move to and fro throughout Forest Hill to find the hearts that were completely His. I also asked God to give me spiritual eyes and ears to discern who He was calling to make this vision and mission a reality at our church.

Seventeen years in ministry had taught me that there are only two things that will last for eternity—the Word of God and people. This certainty instructed me to look for God's answers to my prayers in the form of people, not programs. Programs come and programs go, but the heart of a person seeking to follow God will affect generations to come.

The women's ministry began to take shape and form as God called forth one woman after another whose heart was pregnant with ideas that would bear fruit in the lives of women. With great enthusiasm, these women invited others to join them in what God was doing, and teams began to form. This team ministry philosophy would be foundational at Forest Hill. To this day, if someone wants to start a new ministry, we wait for God to establish a team before beginning.

The first team to form in 1997 was our women's council. The eight women on the council, including me, committed to meet to pray for the women's ministry for one year. The purpose of our time together was to listen to God and wait on Him as He called specific women to purposeful ministry. The single focus of our prayers was that other women would come to know Christ. The majority of our time was spent in praise and thanksgiving, and we kept our prayers short and simple so that each woman had opportunity to join in. Periods of silence didn't concern us as we listened to God. He led us subject by subject as we prayed.

MINISTRY FLESHED OUT IN PRAYER

Remaining in the place of prayer kept us available to join God in what He had purposed. Though we didn't have a master plan for ministry, we came to recognize that the Master Himself had already established the "entry point" of our women's ministry two years earlier through Marilynn Chadwick, wife of our senior pastor. Marilynn is passionate about inspiring and equipping women to reach those who are perishing. Her passion found expression in an idea for a women's event that could impact entire families with the gospel.

"We simply invited our women to bring their unsaved friends to an event we called a supper seminar," recalled Marilynn. "The evening included a beautifully prepared light supper at tables for eight, followed by a biblically based message about 'Discovering Your Children's Gifts.' The night was seasoned with drama, music, and personal interviews with real-life women. It was designed to be a one-time event, punctuated by an offer for women to sign up for follow-up neighborhood Bible studies.

"We were delighted when two hundred attended but expected no more than fifty to show an interest in the follow-up since many were not even churchgoers. Imagine our surprise when the response cards came in, showing that nearly 100 percent of the women desired to be in a follow-up group. At that time we had no way to accommodate that many women in small groups or to provide child care on that scale. After much prayer, we planned four more supper seminars that year while we prayerfully considered how to do follow-up."

This one-time event will soon celebrate its fiftieth dinner. The groups are large enough now for each supper seminar that we offer two identical evenings and accommodate nearly five hundred women each night. Our women have invested so completely in the vision to reach their lost friends that we have served somewhere around eighteen thousand meals. Follow-up classes, Bible studies, and annual retreats, all taught and facilitated by our own women, have developed as follow-up opportunities for our guests—many of whom came through our doors never having owned a Bible.

Though we didn't recognize it immediately, God had been laying the foundation of our women's ministry before the task force gave voice to our goals. Going outside the walls of the church, inviting women to an evening planned for them, and offering a Bible study to those who were interested was the fleshing out of the strategy God would use to change lives for eternity.

Katie Moseley and Jody Allen, two women in our church, took seriously the call to pray for one of their new neighbors, Lisa Pearson. "When my husband and I moved to the South, we met a lot of religious people who tried to get us to go to their church," says Lisa. "We finally made up a name of a church so people would leave us alone. But when we first met our neighbors, the Allens and Moseleys, we knew right away that although they were religious they were different. I never felt pressured by them to go to church. In fact, when I was around them, I felt like I was missing out on something.

"Katie and Jody invited me to a supper seminar and I decided to give it a try. There I quickly realized I was part of something special, so I opened up and decided to take in as much as I could. The words coming out of the speaker's mouth were all the things that were in my head. She too had tried everything to gain control in her life, but found the answer to her struggles in Jesus Christ. I was intrigued and signed up for the follow-up class. There I met other women just like me and realized I wasn't alone. My new friends encouraged me to go to the women's retreat and, after much hesitation, I did. There, on Sunday, March 25, 2001, I accepted Jesus Christ as my Lord and Savior."

God was already at work in Lisa's life, and Jody and Katie were available because they opened their hearts in prayer. Now they have the joy of sharing Lisa's new walk with God in a weekly Bible study. God connects our hearts in relationship when we begin with prayer.

MINISTRY VITALIZED IN PRAYER

That Forest Hill's women's ministry began and took on shape through concerted prayer is unquestionable, but how would we sustain it? More than seeing it sustained, we wanted to see it grow and develop. Again, steadfast, ongoing prayer was the answer. As the ministry grew, so did the needs we saw. We identified one such need for a brief follow-up to the supper seminars—something between the evening's event and the long-term Bible study. Although the temptation was to try to plug the hole with a program, we remained true to our commitment to wait for God to call a person and assemble a team. God answered by birthing an idea in the fertile heart of Renee Swope.

Renee had been coming to the supper seminar with friends and neighbors for more than four years. "I have always loved these events," she says. "Marilynn has a way of sharing stories and asking questions that reveal the secret places of a woman's heart."

Two years ago, Renee decided to create a companion study guide that would take her and other women deeper into the very truths that had been taught in the supper seminars. The study guides were published, more than one thousand were given to women who attended, and Renee used them to teach two different four-week classes. More than forty women attended each time, and Lisa Pearson was one of them.

From these classes Heart to Heart ministry was birthed. Now Renee and an incredible team offer classes in the fall, winter, and spring for women who are seeking God but not quite ready to commit to a long-term Bible study. Instead of plugging the hole with a program, we prayed and God filled it with a woman who loved Him and had a passion for other women to know Him too. (More details of these classes are given in chapter 13.)

THE MEASURE OF A MINISTRY

After beginning every meeting, and meeting every opportunity, with prayer, we have learned that the next step is to just keep praying. As God continues to call forth women for ministry, I am fully convinced of the truth of Psalm 68:11 (NASB), "The women who proclaim the good tidings are a great host." Today our women's ministry consists of more than 150 volunteers included in seventeen teams who press on in this journey to love God and love our neighbors.

At Forest Hill, the staff has a review policy each year where our performance is evaluated by the numbering process from one to five, with five being the best. After my first year as women's director I received a three—I really hadn't done anything that could be measured. We were praying a lot and waiting a lot. I understood the grade. But when I walked out of my evaluation I heard a still small voice tell me that in God's eyes I received a five because I was trusting and depending on Him. Some of the successes that are easily seen today were birthed when there was nothing visible to measure. Trust grows as we wait on Him to bring the fruit from our labors at the place of prayer. Since then, as I prepare for my annual reviews, I ask God these questions: Am I trusting and depending on Him? Am I daily obeying what I know He has called me to do? Am I investing in that which will last for eternity— God's Word and people? Are we loving God and loving our neighbors? Have I yielded at any point to the temptation to measure success by how our programs look or how many women are coming?

From the birth of this ministry . . . to the necessary setting of goals and objectives . . . to the calling forth of women to be the hands, feet, and very heart of God's work . . . to the measurement of success, Forest Hill's Women's Ministry is a seven-year work of prayer in progress.

Mary Ann Ruff serves as Director of Women's Ministry at Forest Hill Church in Charlotte, North Carolina. Since 1993 she has developed a women's ministry that includes Women Under Construction Supper Seminars, Mornings for Mothers, Heart to Heart, On the Job Training (OJT) Bible studies, and many other personal growth ministries. She and her husband, David, who is an Associate Pastor at Forest Hill Church, have three teenage children: Molly, 18; Amy, 16; John, 13. Previously, she served on staff at Colonial Presbyterian Church in Kansas City, Missouri.

SEVEN

CREATING A CONTEMPORARY WOMEN'S MINISTRY

Bobbi Grossmiller and Nancy Schrumm

Fear vs. Faith? Who in his or her right mind would choose to step out in fear when it is possible to step out in faith? We learned in Bible study that faith and fear have a similar definition. Faith is believing that what you cannot see will come to pass. Fear is often believing that what you can see will hurt you, instead of believing God, who cannot be seen. When we were first approached to lead the women's ministry at our church, it was fear that struck us like a bolt of lightning, not faith!

In December 1997, in spite of our more than seven hundred church members, our women's ministry consisted of six elderly ladies. They met monthly for bored meetings; agenda driven, business run, bored meetings. There is no spelling error in the previous sentence. These were boring monthly meetings!

Without continual evaluation, ministries tend to become stifled. It's not intentional. It's that the familiar becomes comfortable, and to look outside the box takes a lot of effort, hard work, and the dreaded vulnerability of failure.

But God had a plan for our growth, and He was patiently waiting for someone to step up to the plate, outside of her comfort zone, and get creative. Isn't it just like God to present us with a study of Matthew 25 at precisely this time? Read the Parable of the Talents in Matthew 25 and then reread it, paying particular attention to verse 25. The first two gentlemen invested what God gave them, but do you remember what the third man did? He hid the talents his master bestowed on him out of fear (v. 25). That was the exact reason we had said no to leading this ministry. But God continued to check our spirits, and we began to question what we were doing with the talents God had given us.

Having recently attended a spiritual gifts assessment class, we realized we could do this. In fact we soon changed our tune to "we get to do this!" Bruce Bugbee, Don Counsins, and Bill Hybels' book *Network* is a wonderful resource that will enable you to become better equipped for the challenge of identifying your strengths. God wants you serving in an area that glorifies Him and brings life to the body of believers. After identifying the gifts that God has given you, it will be exciting and exhilarating to see what God is going to do through you.

Building an effective women's ministry is a great way to minister to a large number of women. The first thing to remember is that women are busy, involved, and often on overload. Your job is to find a way to minister to the total woman without adding any extra stress. The format that has proven successful in our church incorporated a three-point program: Love the women, meet them at their needs, and raise them up in Jesus.

1 Corinthians 12 Woman

Christlike Mind
Romans 12:2

The Word

Tongue of a Disciple
Isaiah 50:4

Ears to Listen
Isaiah 50:5

Shoulder to Cry On
Romans 12:15

Undivided Heart
Jeremiah 29:13

Hands to Serve
Galatians 5:13

Knees
Praying Woman
Luke 18:1

Feet
Ready to Go
the Extra Mile
Matthew 5:41

LOVE THE WOMEN

To borrow a business term, we began networking. Because we didn't know everybody in our church, nor did they know us, we began having intimate coffees and small luncheons. Through our networking we told our excitement about the possibility of what a women's ministry could do not only for the church but also for women in the community. Unfortunately, people buy into the negative thinking of "what's in it for me?" We made our enthusiasm contagious. Women naturally get excited about what their leader is excited about. Loving the women became easy when we taught it through this simple acronym: L.O.V.E. means Listen, be Open-spirited, Validate, Encourage.

L = Listen

Stop doing all the talking and learn some simple techniques for being a better listener. You can do this by reading any good self-help book. Les Giblin's book *Skill with People* is an excellent resource. Before you attend the activity you have planned for the women, think of some questions you can ask that will engage them in meaningful conversation. Then listen! Our husbands, who are businessmen, taught us to use the acronym F.O.R.M. to encourage others to talk about themselves: Family, Occupation, Recreation, Money. Any of these topics are great for breaking the ice and therefore can lead to warm and friendly chats.

Follow-up is vital to being a good listener. As women told us needs, we would make a conscious effort to touch base with them within a week to see how they were doing. A quick phone call or a personal note helped us make a permanent connection, therefore getting to know them better. It's the old saying "No one cares how much you know until they know how much you care" that matters. Through first-hand experience we have found that statement to be true. This helped us as we began to build a team of leaders. By connecting with new women we were able to position them according to their spiritual gifts in all areas of service such as administration, finances, hospitality, missions, prayer, etc.

O = Open-Spirited

Develop a personality that draws people to you. One of our recent speakers told a story about visiting her grandmother at a convalescent center. Her grandmother opened her eyes and said, "Lisa, your face is a present to me." When people see you coming, do they consider your presence a present to them?

Become a people person, one who draws others to you. This requires a high degree of humility. You need to develop honesty, vulnerability, and openness with people. We would use the term *relaxed,* but we've succeeded in building this ministry in spite of being labeled Lucy and Ethel. Our combined eight children laughingly (and lovingly) call us "hyper, type A, jammin' in the fast lane ladies"! You need to become a person who is extremely approachable. As you become more open-spirited, people will naturally want to be with you.

Part of humility is realizing you have weaknesses. Surround yourself with women who are strong in the areas you are weak. Begin to recognize other women's gifts. This is a great time to begin your networking lunches. At this point you can find out who your key players are. Who are your biggest supporters? Who are the movers and shakers? Who is gifted with administrative skills? Who are the extroverts, always out there talking and listening?

Look for areas where newcomers can be involved. Strive to keep the ministry new and rejuvenated. Fresh ideas and insights are always a welcome investment. Concentrate on drawing women in from all areas of the church, such as women involved in children's ministry, those in youth ministry, senior citizens, homemakers, career women, etc. Keep in mind that people will help support what they help create.

V = Validate

This seems to be the buzzword of the decade. We all need to be affirmed. Make it your goal to find something good in everyone, and then be sure to tell the person what you have seen! A few years ago a close friend e-mailed us this story, which really touched our hearts.

"Shine Up Your Neighbor's Halo"
(Author unknown)
One Sunday morning, drowsing in a back pew of a little country church, I dimly heard the old preacher urge his flock to "stop worrying about your own halo and shine up your neighbor's!" It left me sitting

up wide-awake, because it struck me as just about the best eleven-word formula for getting along with people that I've ever heard.

Validation is another way of telling people what is right with them. It supports a deep psychological truth, that people have a tendency to become what you expect them to be. We like to begin our edification from the top: our pastor's wife. What better way to honor a man than to edify his wife? Likewise, what better way to honor a woman than to edify her children?

When our children were little we asked them to memorize Ephesians 4:29, "Do not let any unwholesome talk come out of your mouths, but only what is helpful for building others up according to their needs, that it may benefit those who listen." We had a jar in the kitchen called the 3 Cs. No complaining, no criticizing, no condemning. Anyone caught in the act had to contribute 25¢. We tried to incorporate this within our leadership, teaching women that it's vital to find the good in people and programs.

E = Encourage

It's amazing what can be accomplished for the Lord when we don't care who gets the credit! Encourage creativity! Jesus Himself said: "It is more blessed to give than to receive." Remember your choir days in school when you gleefully sang "The Twelve Days of Christmas"? A creative way to bring joy to someone who has experienced a particularly trying year is through a gift delivery program based on this song. Select twelve women who will work together in blessing a selected recipient. Beginning on December 13 and ending on December 24, one of the twelve women will anonymously deliver a gift along with a personalized note. For example, on the third day you may choose to deliver a set of three picture frames. Likewise, on the twelfth day a dozen roses is a nice touch. Don't limit yourselves to just the Christmas season . . . anytime is the perfect time to bless someone!

Many folks are blessed as they live out the promise of Acts 20:35. Encouragement knows no bounds. It has the capacity to put a smile on someone's face. It can actually change the course of a person's day and perhaps even her life. When all is said and done for us, encouragement was probably the most significant aspect in learning how to love the women.

MEET THEM AT THEIR NEEDS

In the book of James, God says that if a person comes to you and has no food, and you respond by saying, "I'll pray for you," what good is that? The Word tells us to exhibit and overflow with good works. So when a young mother has just had a tonsillectomy, we don't simply stop at patting her on the hand and say we'll pray for healing. We contact our food chain, and they arrange for a few days of soup to be delivered. If one of our leaders is on overload, we don't complain and say "she doesn't have time to spend with me." We get a team together to find a way to lighten her load. How about offering to clean her home, do her laundry, or run her carpools? This was God's intention, that we become aware of a need and we do all we can to meet that need. Teaching women to follow through with that example reaps blessings for both parties!

Make sure you have your finger on the pulse of the women in your fellowship. Begin to assess the dynamics of your women. In other words, to what age groups does your ministry reach out? Are there working women, stay-at-home moms, or home-schooling moms? What are the hobbies and interests of these women? Research your community to find complimentary programs that will minister to these needs. Plan a Saturday brunch at a woman's home. Invite professionals from the community to give a brief lecture on their area of expertise followed by a question and answer period. Choose informative topics such as osteoporosis, nutrition, depression, household organizational skills, creating a babysitting co-op, menopause, budgeting tips, fitness, Pampered Chef demos (with the proceeds going to update your church kitchen), computer instruction 101, 102, etc. The possibilities are endless! When we had illusions of grandeur, we felt we could minister to all the women all the time. Reality soon taught us we could actually minister to most of the women, most of the time. These specialized vignettes addressed the diversity of our women.

One of our ideas was Mom's Day Out. Hands down, this was easily the best *and* the worst event we planned. It was the best because young moms were excited and blessed having a free day of baby-sitting. We created a day full of age-appropriate activities to occupy our moms' preschoolers. Thinking we had the bases covered with plenty of women lined up to help these busy minds and hands keep out of trouble, we never could have imagined the day's events. Then came the worst part: They came! Not only did they come, but they had the audacity to bring their neighbors' kids. We quickly realized our hours of 9:00 to 2:00 were seriously exaggerated. We were completely exhausted after numerous games of ring-around-the-rosie, round after round of tag, and hours of hide-and-seek, not to mention the numerous bathroom calls and diaper changes. These kids were *not even remotely* interested in sitting down to watch a Barney video. But many young moms who don't have family geographically close loved the opportunity to have some down time to spend with friends, go shopping, or just be thankful for a little solitude.

Because you and your team have become good listeners, you will come to know the needs of the women within your congregation. One exciting thing that does unfold is the connecting principle. In *Connecting,* Larry Crabb says, "Ordinary people have the power to change other people's lives. . . . The power is found in connection, that profound meeting when the truest part of one soul meets the emptiest recesses in another and finds something there, when life passes from one to the other."

Connect women! As women's lives and past experiences became known (such as abortion, affairs, rebellious teenagers, medical challenges, etc.), we would attempt to connect them with other women who had encountered similar life experiences. The cardinal rule is to first obtain permission to tell another's story. The reason for connection doesn't always have to be serious. How about connecting two acquaintances who love the same author, or women whose children are in the same sport or activity?

RAISE THEM UP IN JESUS

All the fluff and all the froufrou is what God has used to bring people into the ministry. The ultimate goal is to introduce them to Jesus. Oftentimes Christianity is caught more than taught. We continually provide a wide selection of Bible studies ranging from "Stamping for Jesus" (a weekly group that meets to do the art of stamping and have a short devotional) to an in-depth study of Revelation. Each study is designed to create a hunger and thirst for the Lord.

We have instituted a great prayer group known as "Mugs and Muffins." Once a month women meet to pray for the women of the church, the leadership, the upcoming programs, and any other specific concerns. The home hostess bakes muffins, and everyone brings her own mug. Little prayer, little power. Lots of prayer, lots of power!

It has been proven over and over that most people come to know Jesus from a person with whom they have established a relationship. By building relationships we earn the right to be heard. Before we were saved, we remember running away from "in your face" and confrontational believers! Perhaps that's why our ministry was built by first loving women and meeting them at their needs. "Preach the gospel, and if necessary use words" and "Caught more than taught" were practices brought to life through this ministry. People are always more important than any program. It's encouraging to remember 1 Corinthians 3:6: We can plant, we can water, but God Himself causes the growth!

Jesus wants a relationship with us. Sometimes we complicate the Great Commandment. He tells us very simply yet profoundly . . . love Me and love My people.

In closing, the Lord tells us to never grow weary in well doing. Persevere and be consistent. Practice seeing people through the eyes of God. Our goal in leadership is to raise up women. It's not for the purpose of accomplishing our goals and agenda, but to place women in a position where they are inspired to grow spiritually. You may have heard that in the Kentucky Derby the winning horse actually runs out of oxygen after the first half mile. He goes the rest of the way on heart. Heart is what makes the difference when building an effective women's ministry.

Bobbi Grossmiller has been blessed to be a stay-at-home mom of four while making a "career" of volunteering in her children's schools, their community, and their church. She and Bill, her husband of twenty-five years, live in Bowie, Maryland, with their two youngest children.

Nancy Schrumm, along with her husband, Lew, is currently on staff at Mt. Oak Church as Small Group Coordinator. She and her soul mate Bobbie were instrumental in developing and directing an active and alive women's ministry program. Although a registered nurse by education, her passion is loving and building life into her four children: Amy (now married to Joe with baby Olivia), Tucker, Jeffrey, and Julie. Nancy loves life and lives by Romans 12:11, "Never be lacking in zeal, but keep your spiritual fervor, serving the Lord."

Bobbi and **Nancy** currently lead seminars and workshops training women in leadership positions. It's their desire to see an effective women's ministry firmly planted in every community throughout the country.

E I G H T

PROMOTING YOUR WOMEN'S MINISTRY

Glynnis Whitwer

STEP 1: BUILDING A FIRM FOUNDATION

Beginning with the End in Mind

At the very large and busy university I attended, it was important to complete a Senior Check-Out in one's junior year. This document outlined the courses a student needed to take over the next two to three semesters in order to graduate. Due to its importance, the university encouraged students to complete this document and have it approved by a counselor. It was in a counselor's office that I read a hand-drawn poster that said "Plan Ahead for Your Senior Check-Out." I wasn't impacted by the words as much as the way they were written. They started at the left of the poster in big, bold strokes, but three-quarters of the way across, the letters got smaller and smaller, and eventually curved down the right side of the poster. The writer's point was obvious: Plan ahead.

What an accurate portrayal of so many elements of life and ministry. Many times we begin a project or ministry with the best intentions—our confidence level is high. But as distractions or challenges nudge us off our path, we can wander away from our original intent.

It's a well-known and true axiom, "If you don't know where you are going, how will you know when you get there?" I believe this is true for women's ministry as well. Before beginning any aspect of ministry, it's important to have a plan and to know your purpose. It's important to begin with the end in mind. One of the best ways to accomplish this is to create a mission statement.

Creating a Mission Statement

A mission statement is a critical element of any ministry. Sometimes called a purpose statement, it can be one sentence or a paragraph, so long as it states your goals. It clarifies your purpose for existing. Once complete, it guides your decision making and gets people excited about being in ministry together.

Unlike a business mission statement, which might be influenced by economic trends and profit and loss goals, the mission statement of a Christian ministry should always be guided by the Holy Spirit. The writing of a mission statement starts and ends with seeking the will of the Lord for your church and praying for wisdom and inspiration from the Holy Spirit.

It's important to involve others in the prayer and preparation, so gather a group of women with a heart for the ministry and pray to agreement before finalizing your statement.

Here are some practical tips for creating your women's ministry mission statement:

❧ Answer the question: What does God want for the women in this church?

❧ Review other ministries' mission statements for ideas.

❧ Keep it short and easy to remember.

❧ Have it reflect the values of your church.

❧ Keep it visible—frame it and hang it on your wall and incorporate it into promotional material.

SAMPLE MISSION STATEMENTS

1. Focus on the Family: To cooperate with the Holy Spirit in disseminating the gospel of Jesus Christ to as many people as possible, and, specifically, to accomplish that objective by helping to preserve traditional values and the institution of the family.

2. Proverbs 31 Ministries: Proverbs 31 Ministries is dedicated to glorifying God by touching women's hearts to build godly homes. Through Jesus Christ, we shed light on God's distinctive design for women and the great responsibilities we have been given. With Proverbs 31:10–31 as a guide, we encourage and equip women to practice the Seven Principles of the Proverbs 31 Woman.

3. Mothers Of Preschoolers, International: MOPS, International exists to nurture every mother of preschoolers by meeting her distinct needs to the glory of Jesus Christ.

Communicating Your Vision

If you have written a well-thought-out and prayed-through mission statement, it will spark a flame of hope and excitement in those who hear it. They will see the potential for God to do mighty things through your women's ministry, and they will grasp hold of this vision, making it theirs.

Women hunger to be part of something that has meaning and eternal value. As you communicate your mission statement to the women in your church, they will become a ministry team, able to accomplish much more together than alone.

Using Your Mission Statement as a Planning Guide

Once you have defined the goals for your ministry it is much easier to meet them.

Now as you plan events for the women in your church, use your mission statement as a guide. Identify events that will fulfill the goals of the ministry and schedule them on a calendar. Evaluate where your ministry could be in five years and determine what it will take to get there. The benefit of scheduling events over a period of a year or more is that you develop a "big picture" mentality.

Advance planning also allows you to reach out to women in all stages of life. Start with evaluating the needs of the women in your church. Do you have a lot of young mothers and wise, older women? Consider a mentoring program. Are there women struggling in their marriages? Consider a class on becoming a godly wife. As you are making plans to meet the needs of women, offer programs at a variety of times of day and days of the week. This will allow participation of women employed outside the home and those non-employed.

Another benefit of planning is that you are able to meet needs outside of your church, thus creating a link for many women who might otherwise not visit. Perhaps there is a large population of single mothers in your area. Can you offer a Saturday morning budgeting class, with child care available?

Before scheduling any event or class, consider if it agrees with the mission statement and meets the goals set for the ministry. If it does, proceed with confidence, knowing that you are following the Lord's leading each step of the way.

Planning Each Event

Goal setting is important for individual events and starts with a team approach.

Before planning a specific event, gather the women in your core leadership group and pray for direction. As the Lord sets the agenda, evaluate how this event supports your mission and develop specific goals. Then, as you make decisions, you can refer to your goals. Remember to communicate these goals to all volunteers.

A few years ago, my church had a vision to reach women who did not attend church. After prayer, we agreed that in order to accomplish this we would plan an event that was not on a Sunday or in our main sanctuary. Our goals were for the women in our church to invite friends to a non-threatening, fun event, where they would be encouraged and the Good News would be told. As we reviewed the calendar, we scheduled a Mother's Day Tea and a Christmas Cookie Exchange, and our planning began.

The planning involved a team of women who understood the purpose. As we considered every decision, we kept the goals in mind. From the first impression to what the ladies would take home with them, we considered how to reach someone who didn't currently have a relationship with the Lord.

As we follow the Lord's leading and plan events to minister to women, we need to remember the results are up to Him. Our part is to be obedient—to seek His heart in all we do. We are the planters and the waterers, but God makes things grow (1 Corinthians 3:6). This knowledge releases us from a performance mentality, and puts the focus rightly on the One who deserves all the glory for the things He has done.

STEP 2: PROMOTING
YOUR MINISTRY'S SPECIAL EVENTS

Identifying Your Target Market

You know the truism about the "best laid plans." We can have the most delightful, spiritually enriching events planned for the women in our church, but they need to attend to benefit.

Most of us know numbers don't equal success. It shouldn't matter whether ten or one hundred women show up at our midweek Bible study. We know God values our obedience and looks at our heart's intent.

However, God loves and desires to reach every person on this earth. So while we don't count numbers for bragging rights, we should make every effort to encourage women to participate in the church's events.

I have a degree in journalism and public relations. In school, one of the most helpful concepts we learned was the idea of target markets. In business we ask, "Who is going to buy this product or service?" In ministry, we ask, "Who is going to benefit from this service?" By knowing whom we are trying to reach, we can customize our approach to getting them involved.

Saying that all women are different is an understatement. Not only are women in different life seasons (single, stay-at-home mothers, married—no children, empty nesters, widows), but women have grown up in drastically different generations. We are ministering to women who grew up in the Great Depression, like my mother, and women who are Gen-Xers, like my nieces. Although there's danger in blindly categorizing people, knowing general characteristics about these groups of women gives us an advantage in reaching them for Christ.

Once we have identified our target market, we can proceed with designing a multilayered, creative approach to promoting our programs.

Creating a Multilayered Approach to Promotion

Long gone are the days when you could put an announcement in your Sunday bulletin and ladies would flock to sign up for your conference. On a given Sunday morning you'll find me with bags draped over my shoulder, hands grasping colored pictures, and a brain scrambling to remember who I was going to tell what, all while I'm trying to corral three hopping, skipping boys to the car. And I'm not alone.

Make the best use of your church's promotional avenues, such as the bulletin or announcements, but don't stop there. Today's busy times call for creative approaches to reaching women. Here are some suggestions for ways you can promote the events you've worked so hard to plan:

1. **Newsletter**—I think every church should have a newsletter. It should contain information about the current month's activities, as well as upcoming events. It serves to provide as much information as possible in one place. Once it's complete, get it to all your members and have it available for visitors throughout the month. With the availability of computers and affordable desktop publishing software, anyone who can type can create a newsletter.

2. **Brochures**—Brochures can be as simple as a one-page flyer, or as complicated as an attractively designed tri-fold format. Use a brochure to include information about a single event. Answer as many questions as you can and provide a tear-off registration form if necessary. Unique paper, photos, and clip art add interest to brochures.

3. **Personal Invitations**—Everyone likes to get mail, if it's not a bill. Women especially like mail if it's hand addressed and has a pretty stamp. Gather some volunteers, serve coffee and brownies, and handwrite invitations.

4. **Use E-mail**—Communication via e-mail is growing in popularity. Working women and full-time homemakers are depending on e-mail to stay in touch. What about sending out a weekly notice of upcoming events, complete with a Scripture for the week? This is a great job for a housebound volunteer.

5. **Phone Calls**—A friendly voice on the other end of the phone brings cheer to someone feeling alone and left out. Identify women who are sporadic attendees and invite them using a personal call.

6. **Preprinted Invitations**—Having a preprinted invitation is a great way for women to invite friends who don't attend church to an event. Keep this simple and attractive. Encourage your members to keep several with them at all times, so when an opportunity presents itself, they are prepared.

Promoting Events Outside of Your Church

Local media are often willing to promote events that are open to the public. Although this takes advance planning and a little extra effort, it is an effective and free avenue to broaden your ministry outreach.

Start by making a list of newspapers and radio stations in your area that have a community calendar or a religion section. Make a phone call and record their news deadlines. Some entities need information a few days before publication, while others need several months notice. While on the phone, ask how they prefer to receive news—whether by mail, fax, or e-mail.

Armed with that information, prepare a press release that contains answers to the Five Ws—who, what, where, when, and why. It's best to write it in the simple, straightforward style of a news article, without a lot of hype, and with all five Ws answered in the first paragraph, followed by other text that expands on the basic information.

If you have a photograph that will enhance the story, send it to each publication with the release. This is especially important if your event features a well-known speaker. Photos increase your chances for publication and make the story more interesting.

Another way to reach women outside your congregation is to invite smaller churches to participate. This is a great way to minister to others who may not have organized women's ministries or the space or budget to host an event.

Preparing for Your Event

When I planned special events in the corporate world, we always took a "Do You See What I See?" walk before the big day. A group of us started at the perimeter of our property and walked the path a visitor would take. We took notes of cobwebs, dead leaves, fingerprints on windows, cluttered desks, inadequate signage, etc. We looked at our property with new eyes—trying to see what a first-time guest would see. Then, of course, we swept, cleaned, and organized.

Before your next event, gather your core leadership team and take a similar walk. You only have one chance to make a first impression, and it should be a good one. Think through the questions and concerns that might be held by a woman attending your event and address them. Being prepared allows everyone to relax and enjoy the experience once it begins.

May we never get so wrapped up in the details of planning any event that we neglect the real reasons we do what we do in women's ministry. May we always remember that we are tools in the hands of an Almighty Designer, who works through us to accomplish His purpose of drawing men and women to Himself.

Glynnis Whitwer, with Proverbs 31 Ministries, is the Senior Editor of "The P31 Woman" newsletter. Glynnis worked in public relations for many years, writing promotional materials and organizing special events. She has been a speaker, teacher, and leader in women's ministry at her church. Glynnis has been married to Tod for nineteen years and has three sons, ages seven, nine, and eleven.

HOW TO WORK WITH THE MEN IN YOUR CHURCH

Diane Passno

Have you ever pondered this question, after squabbling with a fellow Christian: "If we love the same Lord, and want to serve Him with the same passion, why can't we just get along together?" It seems disrespectful to the Lord we love to have quarrels and disagreements within the body. Aren't Christians supposed to model Christlike behavior to an unsaved world?

Unfortunately, differences between believers have occurred with great regularity over the centuries, and they continue to occur today, despite our best intentions. One such arena is the "battle between the genders" that has been especially noticeable since the advent of the feminist movement in the 1960s. That conflict has spilled over into the church, and both men and women have struggled with the issue of roles and leadership models.

Although the positions of leadership that I have held have been in a Christian parachurch ministry, which should never be confused with "the church," I have learned some lessons over the years that are worth sharing, if only to prevent other women from going through needless heartache. Some of these lessons sound so simple, when written as words on a page. Yet the actual learning of them has cost me a lot of personal mayhem, most particularly because of my strong will. I've often thought that the Lord must have an incredible sense of humor, placing me with the marriage partner I have, for one thing, and then with the boss I have, for another . . . both of whom have wills of iron! What better way to teach and mold me!

I am making an assumption that you are probably in a position of leadership in your church, whether it be teaching Bible study, leading women's ministry efforts, or instructing toddlers in a Sunday school class. You could also be a deacon charged with visitation or a lay counselor with the responsibility for emotional healing. There are any number of roles that women are asked to fulfill in the church today.

It is my observation that two things are crucial for a woman to be a successful implementer of programming in her church: first, the program she is championing must be the Lord's agenda, not hers, and it must be consistent with Scripture. Sincere Christians can often lead a congregation down bunny trails because their enthusiasm for their own great ideas left the Lord out of the equation.

Second, a woman in any leadership role must learn how to effectively communicate with the senior pastor, the elders, and the business administrator (if there is one) for her program to be successful. If she cannot be the "change agent" because of conflict with these individuals, whether or not she is the source of the problem, then the Lord's purposes will not be accomplished. The Lord uses His people to fulfill His purposes, and if relationship problems are so severe that resolution is impossible, He will use other believers to accomplish His ends. I have seen programs fail in congregations because of this type of interpersonal conflict, only to flourish in a church across town where there was unity of purpose among the senior staff.

LEADERSHIP IN THE LIFE OF CHRIST

The Lord's Word is a fantastic instruction manual for women in leadership. It has wonderful examples of how He used our gender to effect change. Each story related in the Scripture in which women played a role is fodder for individual Bible study: What lessons can we learn from the lives of these women? And what lessons can we learn from the life of Jesus? The model of Christian maturity that we are to portray to our congregations and to the world at large *must* be consistent with how Jesus lived and what He taught.

Although we don't have a photograph of what Jesus looked like physically, we have a wonderful description in the four Gospels of what He was like to be with and what mattered to Him. Matthew 5:1–12, the passage most commonly referred to as the Beatitudes, is a good place to start. Although these verses are Jesus' description of behavioral characteristics that are highly esteemed by the Father, they also model His own behavior while He walked the earth.

We know Jesus was *bold.* We know Jesus had *strength.* We know Jesus spoke with such *wisdom* that people, even some of the religious elite, flocked to hear Him speak. Jesus did what was *righteous* in His Father's sight, despite being "politically incorrect." And yet, the same Man who felt no hesitation about rebuking the leaders of the Jewish community, about overturning the tables in the temple, and about confronting people waist deep in sin instructs us to be *meek,* to be *peacemakers,* to be *merciful* to others, to be *pure,* and to *endure* persecution. Think about it! Are these latter characteristics those that would be touted in a feminist publication on leadership? Doubtful. And are the words I've highlighted inconsistent with one another?

WOMEN'S LEADERSHIP STYLES

It is my observation that women raised in the generation saturated with feminist dogma have a very difficult time understanding how to relate to men in authority because of confusion over gender roles and the concept of "biblical submission." They would be very comfortable with the words *strength* and *boldness* because these are qualities esteemed by the feminist spokesmen of the day . . . women whom they see on television or on the nightly news . . . women who were their college professors. However, *meekness, mercy, purity, peacefulness, enduring*—these words raise the hackles of ardent feminists.

I believe that my own success in relating to men in ministry has been the ability to mesh the seemingly conflicting behavioral characteristics mentioned above. I know that this is a very confusing message to send to women who have been indoctrinated their entire lives with feminist dogma, but it is *to your advantage* to be feminine in the workplace! There are certain innate attributes that make men unique, just as there are characteristics that are uniquely feminine. It doesn't go over well when one gender attempts to emulate the other. Men are much more aggressive and competitive, as a rule, than women, but our gender tends to be much more articulate and sensitive to relationships than men. I have found it much more successful in meetings to rely on my verbal and relationship sensibilities than to try to "duke it out" with my male peers.

I recently had lunch with a well-respected woman pastor in Colorado Springs. She had been brought on staff at a fairly large church to be the children's pastor, which continues to be her title. However, she has earned the respect of the entire pastoral staff by the way she conducts herself in meetings—by being the articulator of great ideas and by being the "relationship" builder among her peers, all men. More and more responsibility has been given to her, including preaching on select Sunday mornings, because she never violated who God made her as a woman. Men just relate better to a feminine woman than a woman who is trying to act like a man in order to be accepted. Although inner strength and boldness are necessary at times, much more can be accomplished by emphasizing those unique traits that make a woman so special and so different from the men she is relating to in the hierarchy of leadership.

One of the reasons I wrote the book *Feminism: Mystique or Mistake?* was to try to communicate to women the difference between a Christian worldview of femininity and the indoctrination they have had over the past forty years by feminist activists. I also wanted to show the Christian underpinnings of the modern feminist movement. Very few women understand that the feminist movement began *within the church, led by Christian women.* Francis Willard, one of the first Christian presidents of the Women's Christian Temperance Union, saw very clearly the issues of inequality that were so pervasive in the 1800s, some of which linger to this day. I consider it an absolute tragedy that the church failed to understand the movement. The result: It was co-opted by the secular world. Christian women need to comprehend that the Lord has a much more "freeing role" for them than our current crop of feminists do, and this includes their role in their local church.

INTERACTING WITH MEN FOR MUTUAL RESPECT

If you are under fifty years of age, you have been raised in a "feminist culture." This culture is completely at odds with the leadership structure of the vast majority of churches. Sparks often fly because of the preponderance of male leadership; women have been taught to question anything that smacks of patriarchy. I hear this so often: "Well, I wasn't able to accomplish what I wanted to do in my ministry to women because the church is so antiquated in the way it views women's issues. And I didn't stand a chance with all those men looking over my shoulder. They just don't get it. I'm treated as a second-class citizen."

When things go awry in your relationships with the men in your congregation, don't succumb to the victim mentality; look inside yourself and reexamine your own behavior and motivations. Although many times the problem is not your fault, it is a very healthy Christian exercise to consider what you may have contributed to the disagreement. When I have a pity party over something that has occurred at work, I have learned, somewhat painfully, upon self-examination, that many times the problem was *me* and not the man who disagreed with me.

Men will only treat women leaders with the respect they accord one another if women play by the same rules. "Rules" should not be confused with "gender roles." There are certain, very healthy ways to interact in meetings, whether they are in a secular or Christian forum, and everyone needs to heed them in order for successful outcomes to occur. To have different rules or expectations for women makes a woman less worthy of the role she has attained because, in actuality, she is being "tolerated."

Ask yourself these questions: Have I been prepared for meetings? Have I established measurements for success for my program that can be assessed at the completion to ascertain if it actually accomplished the goals I said it would accomplish? If my program was a cash drain on the coffers of the church, was this anticipated in the beginning? Will there ever be a positive cash flow? If not, what is there about my program that would make it very desirable for the church to continue despite the cash drain? Have I been overly emotional in meetings with the church leadership so that they have to walk on eggshells when they talk to me? Do I take criticism personally, or do I use it to build a better program? Have I understood the financial restrictions outlined by the business administrator, or do I use those to shoot verbal arrows at other programs, which have been selected for funding?

A woman in leadership needs to rely on those traits that God built into the genetic code of our gender. We have wonderful verbal abilities—use those to garner enthusiasm for what the Lord has called you to do. We were created as "helpmates"—use that ability to come alongside the men at your congregation to help make your church a fantastic place to be. We are able to put feet to vision—use that to carry out the vision of your pastoral staff. If you perceive weaknesses in yourself that keep you from accomplishing all that the Lord has called you to do, then seek help.

One of the women in leadership at Focus on the Family admitted to her male superior, several years ago, that she had a total handle on her responsibilities except in the area of finances. She detested the time during the fiscal year when she had to contend with the budget needs of her department. Together, they developed a plan whereby she attended several basic business finance seminars. She reports to me now, and I gave her a very high rating on her last review in this area. Because she knew it was a weakness, she faced it, and it became a strength.

Gone are the days when service station attendants pumped gas for us ladies so we wouldn't have to have smelly hands or break a nail. Because of the feminist movement, we aren't treated with the same graciousness as yesteryear. This goes for women in the workplace, as well as women who have a significant responsibility at their church. If we are going to "play in the majors," we need to take the responsibility to train for it, just as our male counterparts have done.

Leadership roles are not for everybody, whether you are a man or a woman. I personally think women make wonderful leaders, and my immediate boss, Dr. James Dobson, feels the same way. He loves the contributions that women have made to our management team at Focus on the Family. However, many times the leadership shoe just doesn't fit. Men aggressively seek to move up the ladder and consider themselves a failure if they are unsuccessful in leadership roles. It is my observation that women seem to be more open to using their spiritual gifts in roles where they sense the Lord wants them, whether or not the position has a title. If you've had your fling at leading others and have discovered that it just isn't your cup of tea, don't despair. God has always worked the most miraculous things through those folks who are "invisible"—those folks behind the scenes who are quietly doing the functions in the church that only are noticed if they don't get done! Whatever your role, whatever the Lord has called you to do, run the race with joy—as if you are playing for an audience of One!

Diane Passno, Executive Vice President at Focus on the Family, is a 1968 Alumnus of UCLA. She joined the staff of Focus on the Family twenty years ago and currently has responsibility for several departments within the ministry, including Human Resources, Constituent Response, Counseling, and Women's Ministry.

TEN

PRINCIPLES FOR FEMININE LEADERSHIP

Amy Stephens

Feminine leadership—can the two words exist in the same sentence? Absolutely! What will feminine leadership look like in the twenty-first century? How will we as women further the gospel of Jesus Christ and make a change in our culture? How do we reflect that which is good in our gender so that people are drawn to the saving knowledge of Jesus?

Some women think that to exercise leadership they must look, respond, and behave like men. Unfortunately, that would fall under the heading of *feminist* leadership—viewing leadership in the context of class or victim warfare rather than being empowered by God-given *femininity.* There is literature too numerous to mention on qualities of leadership. However, the body of Christ continues to grapple theologically and practically with the gap between gender study of leadership and its application to Christian worldview. Fortunately, we have an outstanding number of biblical examples of feminine leadership as well as Christian women throughout church history upon whose experiences we can draw.

BIBLICAL FEMININE LEADERS

The Bible gives us great insight into feminine leadership. Women leaders such as Esther, Deborah, and Ruth were unique in personality, talent, and circumstances. Their feminine leadership was about response to God rather than self, giving for the good of others rather than self-fulfillment, and honoring the wisdom and leadership of others rather than standing alone in self-knowledge. Ruth followed the direction of those in authority over her. Deborah ruled as a judge, and Esther influenced a king and saved an entire nation. All are examples of leadership. Both Old and New Testaments embrace women leaders. Acts 2:18 says that God's Spirit will be poured out on his handmaidens and servants. That is you and me! Esther and Deborah held high positions in society, yet influenced in uniquely feminine ways.

We also have examples of ungodly feminine leadership in the example of Jezebel. Jezebel was bright, creative, strong—all leadership qualities. She was also manipulative, selfish, cunning, and reckless. Jezebel followed her gods with great passion—actually being so involved with her "cause" that she had tunnel vision when it came to slaughtering the prophets of Israel. We see examples of Jezebel-like leadership today in the fight over abortion. However, many people mistake strength and zeal for a Jezebel spirit or form of leadership. Not so. Feminine leadership does not mean shrinking back or sitting in submissiveness until someone gives you permission to respond.

Deborah, a powerful judge, ruled in wisdom, not holding back in her beliefs. Esther threw herself before the feet of God, knowing her people were in danger, and took immediate action once the Lord gave her a plan.

Mary responded affirmatively to the angel when told she would carry the Savior of the world, despite all the questions and uncertainty she would face not yet being married. These women were no shrinking violets!

Neither are the women we see profiled in the book *100 Christian Women Who Changed the 20th Century,* by Helen Kooiman Hosier. This book weaves a beautiful tapestry of stories of the humanity, courage, creativity, and giftings of twentieth-century feminine leaders. Hosier says about choosing the leaders for her book: "No one is perfect. . . . Perfection was not the criteria, but love of God and a heartfelt desire to honor and please him and have a heart of concern for others, seeking to follow in Jesus' footsteps, weighed heavily. The walk had to match the talk." Indeed, we see missionaries, writers, teachers, speakers, and political activists all called by God to meet a need. Key to stories in the profiles is the thread of influence these women had on each other's lives:

> For example, Amy Carmichael became Elizabeth Elliot's "spiritual mother," and Amy's life and writings influenced three Grahams—Billy Graham's mother, his wife, Ruth Graham, and Anne Graham Lotz— A. Wetherell Johnson and others. There is a beautiful thread of influence as, for instance, in seeing what Hannah Whitall Smith's writing meant to Catherine Marshall and others, and how Henrietta Mears' godly example influenced Colleen Townsend Evans and Vonette Bright.[1]

THE CHARACTER OF A LEADER

Influence—discipleship, mentoring, writing, speeches, or teaching —whether in the kitchen or the conference hall, women are spreading the good news of Christ in most creative ways. A twenty-first century Christian leader's first job is to motivate women to develop a thriving relationship with Jesus Christ. Second, a good leader helps women identify their giftings, strengths, and weaknesses so that they can maximize their time and energy for the kingdom of God. Third, a leader listens to God's call in her heart and is true to that call.

God has transformed ordinary people to do extraordinary things, but sometimes in daily living that is hard to see. A gifted leader sees a calling on someone's life and motivates and encourages that person to fulfill it. A gifted leader also lends temperance when we want our calling fulfilled *now.* Leadership does not happen alone in a vacuum. That is why being connected to a small, trusted group of believers in accountability, along with being planted in a life-giving church and submitted to the authority and leadership of the pastor, is key to growth and leadership. Women leaders need to have life-giving relationships with other women in and outside their church body to stay spiritually healthy.

In his book *The Making of a Leader,* theologian Dr. J. Robert Clinton says that the greatest challenge of leaders is to develop godly character. "Apart from character—ministry is only religious activity, or even worse, religious business."

Clinton says that integrity is a key factor for leadership. Integrity is being able to check our intentions in order to shape our character. Clinton says that along the way in our growth as leaders we will be tested in a variety of ways (the fire that purifies the gold). Testing of values determines conviction; temptation tests our conviction; conflict will test ministry vision (which tests our faith); persecution will test our steadfastness; tests of allegiance will show loyalty; and the willingness to make restitution will test honesty. Godly leaders do not escape these tests. A leader is one who learns from a test, learns from reproof, learns from mistakes, and creates a proven track record.

Are you a leader of personal conviction or a people-pleaser? A person of deep conviction knows how to stay the course, sacrifice for others, and practice self-control when needed. A people-pleaser will go against personal conviction to please those around her—she is void of true direction, compromises easily, and is loyal only to those who reward pleasing. Throughout your ministry you will be challenged to please people or please God. This isn't to be confused with knowing how to work and get along with others! This is about allowing the need to please others to be your moral compass, rather than knowing who you are and what you are called to do in Christ. How far are you willing to go to develop yourself as a leader and servant of Jesus Christ? There will be pain, there will be sacrifice, and there will also be great joy. Whom do leaders surround themselves with? Hopefully other wise leaders. A leader without accountability is a disaster waiting to happen. If you are a leader who has a ministry that calls for frequent travel, you *must* protect yourself by going out of your way to be connected to pastoral care and accountability. Let wisdom be the hallmark of your ministry. Cry out for wisdom, accept—don't run away from—reproof, and seek wise counsel, and you will grow in leadership.

For women's ministry leaders this would include making sure that the vision for women's ministry is in line with the pastor's vision. Ask your pastor and his wife for guidelines and ideas that reflect their heart for women's ministry. Develop a mission statement for your women's ministry outreach, and ask your pastor to bless that mission statement. Make sure that all of your activities and outreach are in line with the mission and goals of women's ministry, lest you fall into "religious activity." Leadership does not mean you are all things to all people. It means that you know what you are called to do, which is usually beyond your own capacity, drawing you to the feet of Jesus crying for wisdom every day.

Women are often called transformational leaders, in that they are uniquely life-givers, consensus builders, nurturers, administrators, perceivers, wisdom givers, and helpers. Feminists love to portray that feminine softness is tantamount to being an airhead and wimpy. On the contrary, the greatest test of feminine leadership is *not* to lead like men. You lead with a quiet, dignified strength of knowing that the Creator of the universe has called you to your task and shows His great love for you as a woman. Twentieth-century feminine leaders such as Anne Graham Lotz, Corrie ten Boom, Mother Teresa, Ruth Peale, or Janet

Parshall show us that one size does not fit all in effective feminine leadership. None of these women ran from her gender—and none of these women is thought of as leading like men.

Our test of feminine leadership is the degree to which we embrace our gifts and use them for the glory of God and the church. Moving women toward a greater faith and belief in Jesus and challenging them to love their husbands and families, to seek fulfillment in life-giving activities rather than self-fulfillment, and lastly to be faithful disciples of Jesus Christ, is a job crying out for a leader like you!

Amy Stephens is currently the Director of Fresh Ideas Communication & Consulting, specializing in the area of sexuality and culture as it affects women, youth, and families. She founded the Women's Leadership Network, dedicated to promoting leadership development, education, resources, and advocacy for women. Amy is the former manager of Focus on the Family's Public Policy "Made4More" project, which inspires teens to reach their potential through abstinence and character education. Amy represented Focus on the Family during her ten-year tenure on television and radio and wrote articles and opinion editorials for state and national newspapers and magazines. Her successful restructuring of Focus's Youth Culture Department resulted in the Life on the Edge event for parents and teens as well as booklets and the teen radio show *Life on the Edge.* Amy has been a frequent guest on the Focus on the Family broadcast and did weekly guest commentaries for Family News in Focus. Amy lives in Colorado Springs with her two great loves—husband Ron and son Nicholas. She is the author of numerous reports and curricula for youth and adults.

---

[1] Helen Kooiman Hosier, *100 Christian Women Who Changed the 20th Century* (Grand Rapids: Revell, 2000), 15.

[2] J. Robert Clinton, The Making of a Leader (Colorado Springs: NavPress, 1988), 60.

PART THREE

BUILDING A WOMEN'S MINISTRY

Oh, friends, isn't this an exciting journey? We've climbed the high place of getting our own hearts right before the Lord, and we've danced through the details of starting a women's ministry. We know we are doing all this to lead women to the heart of God, but there is a second incredibly important reason for doing all this—connecting women through ties of friendship. "Friendships between women are special. They shape who we are and who we are yet to be. They soothe our tumultuous inner world, fill the emotional gaps in our marriage, and help us remember who we really are. But they may do even more. Scientists now suspect that hanging out with our friends can actually counteract the kind of stomach-quivering stress most of us experience on a daily basis."[1]

"Until this study was published, scientists generally believed that when people experience stress, they trigger a hormonal cascade that revs the body to either stand and fight or flee as fast as possible," explains Laura Cousino Klein, Ph.D., now an assistant professor of biobehavioral health at Pennsylvania State University in State College and one of the UCLA study's authors. "It's an ancient survival mechanism left over from the time we were chased across the planet by saber-toothed tigers." Now the researchers suspect that women have a larger behavioral repertoire than just "fight or flight." In fact, says Dr. Klein, "it seems that when the hormone oxytocin is released as part of the stress response in a woman, it buffers the 'fight or flight' response and encourages her to tend children and gather with other women instead. When she actually engages in this tending or befriending, studies suggest that more oxytocin is released, which further counters stress and produces a calming effect. . . . In fact, the results were so significant, the researchers concluded, that not having a close friend or confidante was as detrimental to your health as smoking or carrying extra weight!"[2]

Wow! Let's go out for doughnuts. Maybe having friends along will counteract any negative health concerns we have about these yummy treats. Yes, friendships are important!

Ecclesiastes 4:10 says, "If one falls down, his friend can help him up. But pity the man who falls and has no one to help him up!" Helping, encouraging, loving, laughing, sharing, and caring are just a few of the many ways friends make life sweeter. There is no better place to make friends who can connect not only heart to heart but also soul to soul than in a women's ministry.

Join me now as we continue leading women to the heart of God by building the incubator through which friends and mentors can be conceived, birthed, and nurtured.

[1] S. E. Taylor, L. C. Klein, B. P. Lewis, T. L. Gruenewald, R. A. R. Gurung, and J. A. Updegraff, "Female Responses to Stress: Tend-and-Befriend, Not Fight-or-Flight," *Psychological Review* (2000), 107(3), 411–29.

[2] Ibid.

BUILDING THE FOUNDATION OF YOUR WOMEN'S MINISTRY ON BIBLICAL PRINCIPLES

Lisa Harper

I love the story of Balaam. Remember him? He's a colorful character in the Old Testament, who—like a lot of men—had serious difficulty with directions! After Balaam missed God's road signs three times, and then added animal cruelty to his ignorance, God put words of rebuke in his donkey's mouth. He could have used a prophet or a priest to reprimand Balaam, but instead He empowered an animal to speak. It kind of puts everything in perspective, doesn't it? Luke tells us that the rocks will cry out if people stop praising God, and Numbers reveals that God used a donkey instead of a man as His messenger!

One of the most important aspects of effective ministry is recognizing that we aren't nearly as essential as we think we are.

Despite the fantastic favor God gives us to work in and for women's ministries, our labor isn't the most critical aspect of our leadership. God may choose to use us as He draws people to Himself, but He isn't *limited* by us. His holy hands are never tied. And if you think God's sovereign plan for His people depends on your performance, you might need to check your theology at the door. It's an incredible thing to be involved in ministry, but we are not indispensable . . . it's not *all up to us.*

I was reminded of that a few years ago when my friend Judy talked me into entering a road race in Denver, Colorado. I didn't really want to run in the race because, although I was a college athlete and have competed in lots of other sports, long distance running has never been one of my strengths. I must have the runner's equivalent of attention deficit disorder, because any distance over three miles is about as pleasant to me as chewing sand. Judy, on the other hand, is a natural distance runner with very long legs and very little body fat. She finished in the top five at the Pike's Peak Marathon (which boasts a field of world-class runners)—where you have to run thirteen and a half miles up Pike's Peak and then turn around and career back down the rocky mountain trail you've just labored up.

Needless to say, Judy and her long-legged, lungs-of-steel buddies were way out of my league! Still, she persisted, saying it would be fun for me to run the race with her (make that *way behind* her), and I could just think of it as a great workout. Plus, she added, I'd get a cute T-shirt . . . and I've always been a sucker for cute T-shirts. So before sunrise on the morning of the race, my alarm went off in Colorado Springs and I groggily rolled out of bed with a feeling of foreboding. Feelings of foreboding at five in the morning should not be ignored.

Judy and I drove to Denver in companionable silence, although she looked chipper—as if she was actually looking forward to what lay ahead—and my face was drawn with a thousand worries. "What if I come in dead last?" "What if I get violently sick during the race and scare innocent children?" "What if the course officials pull me out of the race because they have to reopen the roads to downtown traffic?" By the time we got to the race site, my stomach was in knots. And to make matters worse, it was snowing and I hadn't brought tights or a sweatshirt. I thought that if I could just eat a warm doughnut and drink some hot chocolate, I'd be fine. But I didn't want to be the only person with a number pinned to my shirt wolfing down snacks. So I just shivered and grimaced and waited alongside lots of thin, perky people for the race to begin.

As soon as the starter's pistol sounded, we were off like horses headed for the barn. For a mile or so I was right up there with the front-runners, racing along at a steady clip. I thought that maybe a genetic miracle had taken place in my sleep and I had evolved into an overnight running sensation. But what had actually happened was that the cheering fans lining the downtown section of the racecourse had ignited my competitive pride! I've always performed well in front of a crowd—some people refer to it as "Kodak courage"—so as long as people were cheering, I ran like a sleek, fleet-footed gazelle.

Soon enough, however, the course turned away from downtown Denver and started winding up a steep hill. The roar of the fans faded into the distance until all I could hear were my own ragged breaths. It was wet and cold and miserable. The race wasn't even halfway over, and I was looking for potholes so I could "accidentally" twist my ankle and hobble off the course with some stolen dignity. I was daydreaming of doughnuts and saying to myself that quitting would be more honorable than faking an injury, when I noticed a commotion to my right. I looked over my shoulder and was surprised to see a giant bacon-lettuce-and-tomato sandwich jogging next to me. The meal on wheels was made up of three teenage boys, tied together and wearing huge foam cutouts spray-painted to look just like a BLT. The first boy was dressed like a seven-foot-tall piece of Wonder Bread, trailing a very lifelike leaf of lettuce. The second young man trotted quickly behind him with just his face poking through enormous strips of plastic bacon, glued to a tomato wedge of horror movie proportions. Merrily bringing up the rear was another grinning slice of Wonder Bread slathered in mustard. They were wearing the biggest, most creative costume I'd ever seen at a sporting event. And they were passing me.

I couldn't believe it! I've played college volleyball, raced mountain bikes, and hiked fourteen-thousand-foot mountains; yet here I was, getting beaten by a sandwich! Something stirred deep within my old athletic soul . . . I just couldn't let a food item beat me to the finish line. What would Judy think? What would I tell my grandchildren? My mind narrowed to the desperate, primitive urge to win. I blocked out the cold, cramps, and chocolate croissant cravings and picked up the pace. If this bounding BLT was going to be defeated, it was up to me.

What "ministry sandwiches" are nipping at your heels? Are you disappointed by lackluster attendance at events? Are you desperately trying to create a more entertaining environment to attract more women to your church? Do you have way too many irons in the fire? Are you plagued by some "less than wonderful" women who criticize every move you make? Do you think overcoming these obstacles is all up to you?

Sometimes I do. Just like my vision narrowed to outrunning the sandwich, my vision often narrows to defeating the difficulties in ministry. I block out everything else and pick up the pace because I think I've got to beat my problems on my own. The discordant melody of "grit your teeth and try harder . . . gut it out . . . no pain, no gain" plays over and over in my head. Until, finally, I get so focused on the minutia of my little battles that I forget God's faithfulness. My masochistic mind-set—thinking that *it's all up to me*—causes me to miss His mercy . . . and thus, the whole point of the gospel!

Retreats can be great, and staying up until the wee hours of the morning with your friends is fun, but God's Word is the only thing that doesn't return void. Events, hard work, even a miraculous lack of gossip among the women you work with will not change their lives. Jesus will. Brokenhearted women need to understand God's compassion;

they don't need another commitment to check off on their Palm Pilot—even if it does take place at church.

So the question isn't about how you can work harder or smarter so as to have a huge, cutting-edge women's ministry. The question is, "How can you communicate and illustrate the miracles of God's faithfulness and mercy in your ministry?" And I think the best way to help women recognize and understand God's love for them is to help women fall in love with His Word. There are promises on every page. Jesus Himself said, "This is about Me!" (Remember His dissertation at the end of Luke on the Christology of the Old Testament during a hike on the Emmaus Road?) As evangelical women concerned with and committed to communicating the amazing grace of the gospel, we must make the Holy Writ—the very words Jesus said were written about Him—the heart of our ministries. And in order to refocus and reestablish our ministries on the bedrock of the Bible, we need to remember the purpose for reading it.

PURPOSEFUL PROMISES

One afternoon when I was in high school, Mom told me to clean the tiles around the edge of our pool with bleach. It was hot, and I got really bored scrubbing with my toothbrush and a bottle of bleach, so I started singing. And since I was pretending to be a famous singer, I thought I'd be a lot more beautiful if the faint mustache on my upper lip was bleached blonde. So while I was sloshing bleach on the tile grout, I liberally painted undiluted bleach across my upper lip. The result wasn't pretty. I learned very quickly that a little peach fuzz is much more attractive than scabs. The same bleach that was good for cleaning the pool was dangerous for cleaning my face. Bleach isn't supposed to be used as a homemade beauty balm!

In the same way, Bible studies are devastating and dangerous when women use them as a legalistic measuring device to justify themselves and judge others. I've met way too many women who are defined by the inductive Bible studies they've completed. They're very proud of all the colors they've used to highlight their pages. And they think they're more "holy" than their neighbors because of all the blanks they've filled in. But Jesus rebuked pious, prideful "Bible-bangers" like them in the gospel of John when He said, "You diligently study the Scriptures because you think that by them you possess eternal life. These are the Scriptures that testify about me, yet you refuse to come to me to have life" (John 5:39–40).

Women who cling to the "righteousness" of perfect Bible study attendance and memorized Greek words are missing the whole point. Our lives aren't made whole by homework. Our raging thirst isn't quenched by rules and regulations. The purpose of reading Scripture isn't to justify, judge, or impress anybody else. We read God's Word so we can *know God.* So we can know His purpose for our lives. So we can remember His faithfulness when we're full of fear. Remember His promises when we're about to panic. Remember His mercy when we've made a mistake. The Bible proclaims a history of rescue, restoration, and redemption. It is the Book that gives us life.

Early in the Old Testament we find the incredible story about God's provision of a ram caught in a thicket, His deliverance of the Jews from Egypt and from wandering around in the desert, and the fruition of a promise of a homeland of milk and honey for His people. And then thousands of years later, New Testament records tell the story of God's provision of a Lamb without blemish on a cross, the deliverance for all of us wandering in some kind of wilderness, and the promise of an eternal home with no more crying and no more dying. This entire Word, breathed by God Himself, weaves a story of redemption. It tells and retells the miraculous tale of a God who finds lost sheep and runs toward prodigal children. A God who will not stand to be separated from His beloved children.

"They are not just idle words for you—they are your life" (Deuteronomy 32:47).

PRACTICAL PROMISES

Listed below are some simple suggestions regarding the "how to's" of creating a more biblically based environment wherever God has plopped you.

❧ Try to build everything you do in ministry on a biblical foundation. For example, if you've planned an event that's just for fun—a canoe or ski trip—great! Building friendships is critical if you're trying to create a safe environment—a refuge—to hear the gospel, which is a dangerous message. But consider how you can facilitate natural communication about spiritual things while you're enjoying each other's company. For example, go prepared with a few discussion questions for an informal time at the event focusing on God's creation. While you paddle you could ponder things like, "What are some of the most amazing things you've ever seen in God's creation?" and, "Do you feel closer to God when you're outside like this? Why or why not?"

❧ If you don't already have one, splurge on a set of biblical commentaries (you might want different commentaries/authors for different books or thematic sections of Scripture), along with an exhaustive concordance and a biblical dictionary of Greek and Hebrew (Vine's is good, along with Zondervan's). These teaching helps are so important when it comes to really understanding Scripture and helping others to understand as well. (Some great biblical helps have been formatted into computer programs too, for those of you "techies" who don't want to lug ten-pound books around!)

❧ Ask someone you know who's a captivating Bible teacher—both in communication style and content—to teach a class for women explaining the concepts of biblical history (how the biblical Canon was established) and the basic gist of hermeneutics (how we interpret the Bible). Make sure your church leadership approves of the teacher's theology, and promote the class by calling it something unthreatening like "Everything You Wanted to Know About the Bible but Were Afraid to Ask!"

❧ Sign up for a seminary class (most medium-size towns have seminary extension courses even if they don't have an actual seminary), and bone up on your own comprehension of Scripture. I've always thought the best Bible teachers were even better students. Although our finite minds will never fully comprehend God's infinite truths, His Word is always fresh and refreshing when we study it with eyes and ears that have been opened through His Spirit.

❧ Create a yearly (at least) course/seminar to train Bible teachers. An important facet of developing a ministry with captivating Bible teaching and application is to pray for leaders who feel called by God to teach *and* have the "gift of gab" (natural communicators). Then help equip them to be more effective communicators and Bible teachers. I don't think it's ever a good idea to base your ministry solely on the style and methodology of one person—even if that one person is you. If you're teaching every single week of the year without any assistance, you probably need to establish a team to assist you. They can help teach (maybe at times when you aren't available or on subjects you aren't comfortable with), give input as you develop themes and ideas for upcoming curricula, pray with and for you, and give you much-needed sabbaticals to be alone with God.

We're not nearly as indispensable as we sometimes think we are. God doesn't need us to accomplish His purposes in our respective circles of ministry. It's important for us to remember that it's not all up to us! But it's also important to remember that His love for us (regardless of our position or performance in leadership) is higher and wider and deeper than anything we can imagine. And nothing can separate us from His love. We're more beloved than we ever dreamed of being. God says so: "The Lord is compassionate and gracious, slow to anger, abounding in love. . . . For as high as the heavens are above the earth, so great is his love for those who fear him" (Psalm 103:8, 11).

By the way, I crossed the finish line just ahead of the sandwich. I think their wind resistance gave me a slight edge.

Lisa Harper, formerly the Director of Women's Outreach at Focus on the Family, is a sought-after speaker at conferences and events around the country. She's known for authenticity, humor, and ability to teach and apply deep biblical truths. She has written two books, *Every Woman's Hope* and *Relentless Love,* and contributed to several others, including *Experiencing God in Worship* and *The Dance of Heaven.* Lisa lives in Nashville, where she leads the women's ministry at Christ Presbyterian Church.

TWELVE

STRESS-FREE WOMEN'S MINISTRY

Gayle Haggard

Happy women are strength to any church. The old adage "If Momma ain't happy, ain't nobody happy" is as true in the church as it is in the home. Helping women find contentment in God can be a big job. There are so many issues women carry with them and so many needy women. We, as women's ministry leaders, can wear ourselves out trying to help them. God in His providence must have a way for us to keep ministering for a lifetime, a way we ourselves can grow in strength, happiness, and effectiveness.

Paul charges church leaders in Ephesians 4:11–12 to prepare God's people for works of service, yet far too often the leaders end up doing all of the ministry themselves. Many churches practice this and the believers are not satisfied unless the pastor prays for them or hears all their problems and counsels them. No wonder we have so many burned out pastors and pastors' families.

Several years ago my husband, who is a pastor, took this Scripture to heart and decided to refocus his sermons and ministry on equipping the people in our church to minister to others. He started what have now come to be known as free-market small groups.[1] These encourage people to gather around some form of common ground, such as interest areas, friendships, or needs, and meet on a regular basis to grow in relationships and to mature in Christ together.

At the time my husband was developing these ideas, I was feeling God leading me to restructure our women's ministry. In order to keep it in the flow of what the church was doing, I looked for ways we could develop our women's ministry into small groups.

We started with ten women's groups, and it didn't take us long to discover we had stumbled onto a really great idea. We found women connecting on a level they never could in a large meeting. Our leaders started telling testimonies of women opening up and sharing their lives with each other. In these settings, they would receive prayer and encouragement. It was affecting their lives and the lives of their families. The small group leaders were ecstatic that God was using them to minister to these women, and they in turn were training the women in their groups to minister to one another.

By the second semester, our number of small groups had more than doubled. More women wanted to minister to others, and many had received training in their previous small groups. I could see my role emerging as the team builder of all these women who wanted to minister to other women. Clearly, my function was to keep them encouraged. This was not hard because of the enthusiasm they were feeling about God's using them to minister to others.

In five years, we have grown to more than one hundred small groups in our women's ministry. These are just the groups focused solely on ministry to women. Our church is healthy, happy, and active, and as the women's ministry coordinator, I couldn't be enjoying ministry more.

Why? Because I am a part of a bigger team. We share a common goal of ministering to women, and we are in this together. Jesus built a ministry team, His disciples, and I would imagine that made His ministry all the more enjoyable and effective. We are strength to each other. We lift each other's burdens; no one has too much to carry or to do. We help each other. And we have the momentum of belonging to a group that has a worthy purpose.

Our mission statement in our women's ministry says, "Our purpose is to connect women in order to help them grow to maturity in Christ." All of our women's small group leaders have this goal in mind. And each of them is connected to a bigger group that is trying to do the same thing. Our hearts are passionate about wanting God to use us to help women. This is not just my passion; I share it with more than a hundred other women.

CONNECTING WOMEN

So why is it so important to connect women? It has taken me many years to understand this, but I've finally come to the conclusion that women really do need each other. Scripture tells us this. Titus 2:4–5 states that older women should teach younger women. There are certain things women need to learn from each other.

But I also think there is another reason. I think women are strength to one another and really help each other in life.

Recently I was asked the question, "Do you talk to your husband about everything?" My response was, "Of course. I mean, I keep no secrets from my husband. OK, the truth is my husband does not always want to talk about everything I want to talk about." Certainly, my husband and I *can* talk about everything and *do* talk about most things;

however, I've learned there are certain things that I am interested in that are not high on his interest list.

It has taken me years to accept this fact. Being the romantic that I am, I want to talk about and do absolutely everything with my husband. But there are a few things my husband would prefer I do without him. It's true there are differences between men and women. This does not diminish our compatibility. If we figure this out and work with it, it's a source of great compatibility. God intended it this way. We are alike yet different. Marriage has the potential for being the most intimate and fulfilling of all relationships because of this. It is also the picture God gives us to portray our relationship with Him.

Yet there appears to be something missing in many women's lives, even those of women in the body of Christ. What is becoming increasingly evident is that women have a need for each other. By opening the doors of our hearts to other women, we can help each other become better women.

However, in our city I've noticed women tend to be isolated from each other. Some unseen force seems to work at keeping women apart. More women than would ever admit to it just do not like other women. Some are afraid of other women and feel they must compete; others are not trusting, thinking they must protect themselves; and still others have bought into the belief that women are silly and mindless and not as interesting as men. I certainly don't want to be seen that way as a woman, and I hope you don't either.

Nonetheless, I was one of those isolated women for many years. I was a committed wife and mother and didn't feel I had the time or need for other women in my life. Without realizing it, I slowly became a dry well. In my ignorance I had cut myself off from the river of women's relationships that was meant to fill me up. Certainly God was my strength, and He filled me up in times of prayer, yet I was missing out on another channel He wanted to use to strengthen my life, and that was other women in the body of Christ. I needed other women to love me, affirm me, and encourage me so that I could love others, and my husband and children in particular, out of a well overflowing with fresh water. I discovered that friendships with other women would not just be a nice addition to my life when I had more time, but I needed them now.

God gives us beautiful pictures in Scripture of what women do for each other. Consider Mary and Elizabeth. Mary was a young woman chosen by God to carry and give birth to the most wonderful miracle of all time. Mary was a ponderer, which means she held things deep inside. Think of all the wonder, joy, ecstasy, fear, and knowledge pent up within her. I'm sure she felt she would burst. She needed to discuss this with someone. But who? Whom could she trust? Who would understand? Certainly Joseph played his role well. He treated her kindly. He too heard from God and protected her. But who could really understand the feminine intricacies of her situation?

There was one. There was Elizabeth. God gave Mary another woman in similar circumstance. Elizabeth was also carrying a child with divine purpose revealed by an angel. She too felt alone. Zechariah couldn't speak. God gave them each other, Mary and Elizabeth. They understood and affirmed what each one was experiencing. They rejoiced in God together and strengthened each other for their tasks.

That's what we women do for each other. We strengthen each other and help each other become better, godlier women. That's why we need to connect with each other.

It's not enough to bring women together in a large meeting. Many of us know it's possible to be loneliest in a crowd. We need instead to provide a way for women to connect on a deeper, more intimate level, heart to heart, so they can get their needs met. We can do this in small groups. In them women can really meet each other, and there relationships can grow.

HELPING WOMEN GROW TO MATURITY IN CHRIST

So how can you be sure once these women connect that they will grow in spiritual maturity?

First I must explain what our free-market small groups look like in our women's ministry. The idea behind free-market small groups is that you let the market (or the women in your church) decide whether an idea for a small group is a good one or not. If people feel it meets a need, or addresses an interest, or has people in it they want to be with, then they will come. So the leader has the freedom to offer whatever type of small group she would like. Our women's small groups include Bible studies, book studies, prayer meetings, tea parties, cooking classes, quilting classes, child-rearing studies, hiking groups, art groups, Christian aerobics, scrapbooking, and many more. We even had a group of women meeting to cross country ski together. These are just a sampling of the many ideas women think of to minister to other women. The goal of the leader, whether she is leading a scrapbooking group or a Bible study, is to help the women in her group mature in Christ. She helps them to connect with one another so they are comfortable, and then initiates discussion, prayer, or study to help the women grow in relationship with God and to learn to help and encourage one another. A leader can do this in a kitchen or on a hiking trail. She just has to give women the opportunity to do it and keep in mind that her goal is to help them develop in God.

Some of our groups are evangelistic in nature. One of my favorite ideas that some of our women came up with was to canvass their neighborhoods with invitations to a "get to know you" coffee or tea in their homes. Some sent out up to fifty invitations in their neighborhood. Usually twenty to twenty-five women would respond.

During the first gathering they would have refreshments and take time to get to know each other. If that went well, they would end by saying, "Let's do this again next month." After one or two gatherings, they would say, "Why don't we keep meeting? Would anyone be interested in studying a Christian book together or doing a Bible study or even a cooking class?" Often ten to fifteen women would respond, and they would form a small group. Sometimes women would respond to attending a Bible study just out of curiosity. They felt safe and comfortable with the leader at this point and just wanted to do something to continue meeting with the other women. Often women would meet the Lord in these meetings, and then the leader would introduce them to the church. Some of the women who are now leading small groups in our church met the Lord in one of these meetings.

We also have small groups that are focused on new believers or mature believers, and plenty that are a mixture. Some cater to single women, widowed women, or married women, but most include women who are in different seasons and stations of life because we have so much we can learn from each other.

We never hear complaints that our women's ministry is cliquish or made up of gossip groups. One reason is that there is something for everyone. Another is that our leaders are godly women who are purposeful in wanting to serve other women and to help them grow in God.

PROVIDING STRESS-FREE LEADERSHIP

Now, how is small group ministry stress free for the leader? Remember your focus is on building, equipping, and encouraging your team of leaders. You pray for and minister to them, and they pray for and minister to the women in their groups. By ministry team, I do not mean a worship leader, event coordinator, prayer leader, and refreshment provider. I mean women who are joined with you in discipling other women. There is great strength in the team; no one person has to carry the whole weight by herself. Another benefit is that you will find your counseling load diminish dramatically as women begin ministering to each other. After all, most women's greatest problem is that they are lonely. A woman's need for love, acceptance, and friendship is met in her small group. Also women bring their combined knowledge and experiences into their groups and find they have the resources among themselves to minister to each other. As the women's ministry leader, you must prepare yourself not to be needed so much.

Something you might want to communicate to your pastor is the benefit to the church of women building long-term relationships. This helps the church to grow and to be healthy. He might also like to know that your goal in women's ministry, other than connecting women and helping them to grow to maturity in Christ, is that the women would be a strength and a blessing to the church as they grow healthy in relationships and spiritual maturity. Let him know the women's ministry is there to serve his vision for the church. Help him to see that you're there to be a blessing to him.

How does our women's ministry work? First we had to recruit our leaders. Our first ones were women I knew who were already involved in serving women. From then on they came from the existing groups, by recommendation of their leaders and by application. We have a process for this to make sure we're not placing practicing criminals and heretics in positions of leadership. But we are also not too constraining here. Remember God uses all kinds of people. The goal is to equip the believers for works of ministry. We have a system for oversight in place to encourage them along the way.

Our women's ministry looks like this: I am the director; I work with two assistant leaders, who each oversee five to ten section leaders, who each oversee five to ten small group leaders. Our small group leaders meet regularly with their section leaders for prayer and coaching in ministry. Our section leaders meet regularly with my assistant leaders for the same. And I meet regularly with my assistant leaders.

Also I meet once a month with all of the small group leaders together for training, vision casting, and team building. I always encourage them that we are a team and our purpose is to connect women so we can help them grow to maturity in Christ.

Since we operate on a semester system, women can join a new small group each semester or stay with their old one. Our women love this system. The testimonies abound of hearts healed, marriages healed, women's lives changed, and friendships formed. Am I stressed? No! I couldn't be enjoying myself more.

Gayle Haggard is the wife of Ted Haggard, who pastors New Life Church, a seven-thousand-member congregation located in Colorado Springs. As Director of Women's Ministry, Gayle helps lead more than one hundred small groups in genuinely knowing the Lord and discovering the strength they can bring to the body of Christ as mature, godly women.

---

[1] For more information on free-market small groups see Ted Haggard, *Dog Training, Fly Fishing, and Sharing Christ in the 21st Century* (Nashville: Nelson, 2002).

THIRTEEN

THE JOURNEY OF A WOMAN'S HEART

Renee Swope

The journey of a woman's heart winds along a path well worn by fellow travelers. Sadly, many women feel alone. Our churches and communities are filled with women who have become isolated in their journeys and haven't the vaguest idea of where they are headed. Few have a map, and some who started with one have lost it or have become too stubborn to use it.

The journey of my heart has taken me through many valleys, peaks, deserts, and streams. For the first twenty-two years I traveled alone and weathered life's storms without the protective covering and guidance of my heavenly Father. I had no map and traveled in circles until I finally gave in one rainy weekend at a church retreat. I remember praying a simple prayer that went like this, "God, I cannot do this any more. Please come into my life and take over. I surrender my life to You."

I had tried to fill a huge vacancy in my heart with everything but God. Turning to people for my value, I found my security and identity in their approval. But no matter how hard I tried or how much I had, it was never enough. I was searching for something, but I didn't know what it was and I didn't know where to find it.

Now, thirteen years later, after serving in women's ministry with college girls, single women, young mothers, working women, and empty nesters, I see that this is the journey of every woman's heart. We are all on the same pilgrimage looking for meaning and purpose, searching for love and intimacy. We try to fill the empty places of our hearts with men, work, children, friends, clothes, food, alcohol, drugs, exercise, and countless other people or things. But it won't work. As Jesus told the woman at the well in John 4:10–14, nothing can satisfy the thirst of our souls except Living Water. And the only place we will find Living Water is in the well of God's heart. How can we make sure the journey of our heart leads us there? How can we lead other women there as well?

JOY IN THE JOURNEY: A FEW TRAVELING TIPS

Although I love spontaneity, my best traveling experiences have been those that happened when I planned in advance and followed a few principles that I had learned from seasoned travelers. Here are a few tips that will bring joy to our journeys on the road and the journeys of our heart: always use a map, be sure to get directions from someone who has been there before, never travel alone, stop to ask for help if you get lost, create an itinerary, and make accommodations for little travelers.

The first thing women need for their spiritual journey is the map of God's Word and the directions He left for us. When I am traveling on the road, my favorite place to buy a map and get directions is a gas station because I can refuel there too. Bible studies and small groups are some of the gas stations in our spiritual journey. Although they do not replace the importance of individual prayer and the studying of God's Word, Bible studies are designated times to pull over and refuel our tanks with "living oil," get more detailed directions when needed, and refresh our souls with prayer in the fellowship of other believers.

The second and most influential necessity for a woman's journey is traveling companions. We were not designed to travel alone. Beth Moore says as women "we long to find someone who has been where we've been, who shares our fragile places, who sees our sunsets with the same shades of blue."[1] Bible studies, small groups, and classes offered in the church provide the setting for women to find traveling companions and ask for directions along the way.

An itinerary is designed to chart out our journey and allow us to evaluate our progress toward our desired destination. A small group itinerary is often referred to as a commitment. It is a written agreement developed by each small group to reflect the purpose and format of its time together. It should include the primary building blocks of the group such as Bible study, prayer, fellowship, service, outreach, and fun. It should also state the meeting time and the duration of their commitment to be together. It is a good idea to create a new itinerary (small group commitment) every six to nine months. Small groups should develop their own itinerary and format, giving independence and individuality to their group, while incorporating the overall purpose of your women's ministry.

To enjoy the journey, mothers will need special accommodations for their little travelers. Moms need to feel comfortable leaving their children in reliable, responsible child care before they can relax in their groups. Child-care workers must be trained, loved, encouraged, and appreciated. Your church can accommodate the need for child care by offering small groups during evening services while child care is available. Some churches have morning groups and hire child-care workers.

Child care can be the biggest obstacle in developing a women's ministry, but it's worth the effort.

At Forest Hill, we have seen the importance of developing a women's ministry that merges with the path of a woman's heart no matter where she is on her spiritual journey. Whether she is a seeker uncomfortable with traditional church settings, a working woman, a stay-at-home mother, or a woman simply seeking to meet with other women, we have created a place for her to connect and grow. Let's look at the unique roles woman have and how the bends in the road for them might help shape the design of your church's women's ministry.

Ministering to Women in the Workplace

In 1994 we moved to Virginia and I became the provider for our family while my husband completed his degree. We joined a church and attended a small group for couples. Although I enjoyed the fellowship and Bible discussion, I yearned to connect with other women who could help me find balance with work and my role as a wife. In the church, I found co-ed Sunday school classes, daytime groups for mothers, and marriage seminars. However, there was little available for working women.

The needs of working women are often overlooked by churches. Mary Reitano directs OJT: On the Job Training, a ministry to women in the workplace. She and her team are meeting a unique need and enjoying the fruit of their labor as they watch women flourish in their walk with the Lord and their relationships at work and home.

"Most working women enjoy using their God-given skills, serving others, being mentally sharp, dealing with people and accomplishing goals. Many love their jobs. However, working women experience a lot of stress, especially working mothers. Often, their work at home and in the workplace is a labor of love for their families. A single working mother is exhausted and usually not working by choice, but out of necessity."[2] The older career woman without a family struggles to find her place at church. All of these women face temptations and challenges in the workplace that create a hunger for God's guidance and a need to connect with others who share their struggles.

OJT was conceived when Mary and five other women gathered to pray and discovered that God was calling them to minister to the working women of their community. After much prayer and discussion, they named their ministry, developed their mission statement, and formed an evening group for working women. OJT now includes ten small groups, a newsletter, and two annual events, affecting several hundred people each year inside and outside the church.

Shannon Senna experienced a richer walk with the Lord and felt a greater sense of purpose when her perspective of work changed from a "job" to a "calling." After helping choose OJT's ministry verse, Colossians 3:23, "Whatever you do, work at it with all your heart, as working for the Lord, not for men," Shannon felt called to put it to practical use. "It was amazing to see God turn my job into a ministry, without me compromising my HR position. I have been blessed to see two of my co-workers come to faith in Christ," Shannon told me recently.

Flexibility is also important in building strong relationships and a strong ministry for working women. These women have many deadlines and time crunches. To meet the need for a relaxed routine after work, OJT small groups meet every other week. To prevent burnout, leaders are encouraged to rotate their role as facilitator every three to six months. To make the workload manageable, a slower pace is taken to complete Bible studies. Special events are offered at convenient times, such as Saturday breakfast or evening desserts, and vary to meet the needs of different schedules.

A working woman needs to be affirmed in her role. When she sees her career as a calling, she can serve the Lord in the mission field of her workplace. Knowing the hours invested at work have eternal significance, she'll gain the strength she needs when bombarded with deadlines, doubt, and discouragement. A ministry uniquely designed for her will affirm that God has gifted her to serve her community in the workplace.

Ministering to Mothers

How can we minister to the hearts of mothers? Soon after becoming a mother, the realization hit that training in childbirth classes was going to provide little help in navigating my tiny fleet through the rocky seas of life. As a mother I knew my role was to be like a lighthouse, whose lamp does not go out at night, and that I would need "living oil" to keep burning, even when I was completely burned out. The consistency and accountability of a Bible study group with other mothers who encouraged me in my relationship with the Lord and my roles as wife and mother helped me keep my fuel line connected.

The responsibility of motherhood brings many challenges. Mothers are busy and tired, both physically and mentally. It is easy for a mother to allow her time with the Lord to creep to the bottom of her "to do" list. Especially in the early stages of parenting, a mother's relationship with the Lord needs extra nurturing. As she faces changes in her roles, her relationships, and her routine, the church can provide the spiritual nutrients she'll need to strengthen her roots during this growing season.

Lisa Allen, Director of Mornings For Mothers (MFM) Ministry at Forest Hill Church, knows firsthand that a mother's heart is fertile soil for the seeds of God's Word. "Most women (even those who've never attended church or Bible studies) are 'spiritually tender' once they become a mother. Looking into the eyes of your child, you realize the importance of your role in forming their values, morals, character, and view of God. Suddenly, you look at your own relationship with God in a whole new light."[3]

A common struggle for many mothers is a loss of identity. A mother can quickly fall into the trap of looking to her performance as a mom to give her the significance she longs for. After the birth of her first child, Lisa grew exhausted by the constant competition and comparison with other mothers and children. Having left the measurable success and satisfaction of corporate life, Lisa began to measure her worth as a mom by the standards of other mothers. She has now taken what seemed to be a stumbling block for her and made it into a building block for others. In her ministry to mothers, she is able to point them to the One who truly determines their worth.

Mornings For Mothers is primarily geared to mothers who either stay home with their children part- to full-time or have a flexible work schedule that allows them to attend a morning Bible study. The ministry's purpose is to bring women together in groups of eight to twelve to study God's Word, remind each other of His truth, support one another in prayer and friendship, and plan times to serve others together.

Lisa Murray, a mother of two, had been in an MFM group for five years. It wasn't until she was away from her group that she realized what a lifeline it had been. "After the birth of my second child I took a six-month break from my mothers' group. I never realized how much I needed to be with other moms seeking to know God and His truth until I was alone. Being involved once again has been like refreshing water for my soul. As I share my joys as well as my struggles with my group, I know that I am not alone. Traveling down the road of motherhood is much more fun when you are walking with God and some special friends."

A ministry for mothers can provide the opportunity for young moms to meet and be mentored by other women who have walked a similar path and gained spiritual wisdom and practical insight along the way. It is a time when they can talk without interruptions and pray without interference. A ministry for mothers also provides a safe place to come for renewal and refreshment. It tells a mom she is important, that her role is valued by God and the church, and it encourages her to look to her heavenly Father as she seeks to be a godly mother.

Ministering to Spiritually Seeking Women

Some women are seeking to know more about the heart of God, but not yet ready to come to church or Sunday school. Many women won't commit to a small group Bible study, but they are willing to attend a dinner or an informal class with a friend. How can we create a ministry that meets spiritually seeking women where they are and ushers them down the path that leads to the heart of God?

One way we have found to effectively minister to spiritually seeking women is by hosting supper seminars (as discussed in chapter 6). These dinners give the women of our church an opportunity to bring friends, co-workers, and neighbors to hear a speaker and be introduced to the gospel in a non-threatening setting.

Heart to Heart ministry was birthed as a next step for the women attending the supper seminars. Heart to Heart classes are designed to help women discover that God cares for their everyday concerns and wants to meet their everyday needs. The format is a four-week study with an open-seminar style covering topics relevant to women, such as contentment, control, anxiety, and hope. Once again, the Bible is introduced through life stories and profiles of biblical characters. A speaker/teacher introduces the topic through her life story and then offers personal reflection questions for the women to discuss in their groups. The speaker allows fifteen to twenty minutes for interaction and then pulls the class back together for further teaching. The classes are designed to allow for two to three discussion sets and last an hour and a half. We offer these classes on Wednesday nights when child care is available.

The setting of the class includes tables of six, dessert and coffee, and a casual environment with lots of interaction. Each table is hosted by two leaders who have been trained to facilitate discussion and point these women to God's Word for answers to their questions.

The purpose of Heart to Heart is that women "may be encouraged in heart and united in love, so that they may have the full riches of complete understanding, in order that they may know the mystery of God, namely, Christ, in whom are hidden all the treasures of wisdom and knowledge" (Colossians 2:2–3). I have had the privilege of watching our ministry verse come to life in Amy.* Her story is a reflection of what we hope women will experience through Heart to Heart.

The wife of a nonbelieving husband, Amy visited Forest Hill by herself eighteen months ago. After attending a supper seminar and receiving a study guide with an invitation to the four-week class, Amy decided to visit Heart to Heart. I remember seeing Amy that first night. Her countenance was heavy and her eyes were distant. As the teacher, I float to different groups each session so I can hear women's stories. Tears streamed down her face as Amy opened her heart. She had just remarried, moved to the United States, and uprooted her children. Her kids hated life here, and she was sure she'd made a huge mistake.

The women in her group listened, encouraged her, gave her Scripture for comfort, and prayed with her before the evening ended. Amy continued to come for four weeks, and when the class ended, she and a few women from her group started a twelve-week Bible study. Amy joined an OJT group last fall and committed her life to Christ recently. Her daughter also started coming to Forest Hill and gave her life to Christ last summer.

Heart to Heart classes are a starting point. And our hope is that once women like Amy have attended the classes they want to find out more about God and will have begun to enjoy the companionship of other women. Our goal is to usher them to the next step in their spiritual journey and help them connect to more spiritually mature

---

* Name has been changed to protect anonymity.

women who can walk with them further in their search for the heart of God.

CLOSING THOUGHTS

By looking at a woman's unique roles and developing a women's ministry that merges with the path of a woman's heart, we can create a place for her to connect and grow. As leaders, we can provide some essentials for her spiritual pilgrimage. Through Bible studies, speaker series, and seeker-sensitive classes we can direct women to the map of God's Word. By carving out weekly times for women to gather, study God's Word, and pray in small groups, we allow them to stop and refuel. By emphasizing relationships we can encourage women to get directions from others who have gone before them and to never travel alone. By developing ministry mission statements, choosing foundational Scripture verses, and writing group itineraries, we demonstrate the importance of having a plan so we can evaluate along the way and make sure we are heading toward our desired destination.

No matter where a woman is on her spiritual journey, we can meet her there. We can take her hand and lead her heart. We can bring her to the well and show her where to find Living Water as we journey with her toward the heart of God.

---

[1] Beth Moore, *Things Pondered* (Nashville: Broadman & Holman, 1997), 7.

[2] Interview with Mary Reitano, 17 December 2001.

[3] Interview with Lisa Allen, 13 December 2001.

THE SEVEN Cs OF HIGHLY EFFECTIVE MINISTRY FOR WOMEN

Christ-Centered

The most important thing we can do to build a life-giving ministry is to make sure it is Christ-centered. The primary building block must be an ongoing connection with Christ through Bible study and prayer.

Coleaders

When Jesus sent the seventy-two out to do ministry, He sent them in pairs. When we serve with a coleader, we are able to better meet the needs of our groups through a balance of personalities and spiritual gifts.

Cultivation

Cultivate New Life. Just as a farmer cultivates the land to prepare the soil for growing future crops, leaders need to cultivate the soil of their women's hearts to prepare the way for more ladies to come into community. Encourage women to invite newcomers to their groups.

Cultivate New Leaders. The best place to cultivate new leaders is within. As members mature in a ministry group, encourage them to birth another group from within.

Commitment

A small-group commitment is a written agreement developed by ministry groups to reflect their purpose and format. Groups should develop their own contract or itinerary, giving independence and individuality to their group, while incorporating the overall purpose of their women's ministry.

Curriculum

In choosing curriculum, many things need to be considered. To make this decision easier, it is helpful to provide a "curriculum list" of book reviews written by leaders assessing the text they've covered, how much work it entailed, whether it fostered good discussions, and whether they would recommend it to others.

Communication

As with any relationship, strong lines of communication are essential in ministering to women. Seek feedback from women in your church through surveys, newsletters, and conversations. Encourage leaders to listen to women's needs and prayerfully consider their requests.

Child care

Some churches accommodate the need for child care by offering ministry groups during the church's evening service while child care is available. Other churches have morning groups and hire child care workers. Child care can be the biggest obstacle in developing a women's ministry, but it's worth the effort.

Renee Swope has served in women's ministry for the past thirteen years and is Director of Heart to Heart Ministry at Forest Hill Church in Charlotte, North Carolina. She is a graduate of Florence Littauer's CLASS (Christian Leaders, Authors and Speakers Seminar) and a certified speaker for The Proverbs 31 Ministries. Renee has written two Bible studies and has been published in "The P31 Woman" newsletter and the *Best of Proverbs 31 Ministry* book. She and her husband, J. J., have been married nine years and have two sons, Joshua and Andrew. They are the founders of It Starts In The Heart Ministry.

FOURTEEN

WOMEN MENTORING WOMEN

Bobbi Grossmiller and Nancy Schrumm

Two weeks prior to Mother's Day we tried to get out of it. Our senior pastor, having more faith and confidence in us than we had in ourselves, said, "I want you to do this." Since he was a calm and usually mild mannered gentleman, this snapped us to attention. We had to deliver the Mother's Day Sunday morning message entitled "How to Be a Great Mom."

Operating totally out of obedience, and after much prayer, we delivered our talk. We told stories about how much we loved being mothers and combined them with a lot of humor and great failure and success stories. We closed by talking about how we felt the Lord was leading us to minister to younger women. We thought perhaps we could meet and discuss, one on one, things that they may have missed growing up. Our model was

Titus 2. We openly challenged the ladies in our congregation to be mentored if they had missed a few basics along the way. Rather randomly, we asked them to sign up for this mentoring program by indicating W.O.W. on our Keeping in Touch cards. (We made up this name to stand for Wise Older Women.)

Thinking that possibly a few women would come forth, we were shocked the following day when the church secretary called to inform us that more than sixty women expressed a desire to be mentored.

The ongoing dilemma is that in the past few years we have had so few ladies volunteer to be mentors. A large portion of our congregation consists of young mothers or women in their forties and fifties who openly confess to not having a lot of spiritual background (no deep roots). We had already made the challenge; now we needed to come up with a solution. Pray, pray, pray! Standing on the promise of Ephesians 3:20 that our God could do exceedingly and abundantly more than we could ever think, ask, imagine, or dream, we forged ahead with our plans.

A wise older woman named Penny, who mentors to the max, loaned us the book *Apples of Gold*. The timing seemed to be a God thing! The author, Betty Huizenga, offered precise study topics for young women and included the idea of building the study around meal plans. This was almost the same format we had in mind. We were thrilled when Penny offered to partner with us in creating our own version of Betty's book. Penny, a self-proclaimed earth mother, worked diligently in preparing simple recipes.

CREATING THE PROGRAM

It was our desire to create a program that ministered to the exact needs of the women in our church. We prayed that the Lord would raise up some new teachers and mentors, as well as some old pros, who would be willing to write each lesson from scratch. We also needed women gifted in administration to organize the entire program. In our case we had Heather, our young mother who delighted in detail. She organized, typed, and orchestrated as we spewed orders and assignments. Through her efforts our young moms had a complete and detailed account of the entire program, from the mentors' bios to the lesson plans and all the recipes.

So we began speaking of our need to our friends, who spoke of it to other friends. This is where our year of networking (see chapter 7) paid off. Most of the women we spoke with felt insecure and ill-equipped to mentor, but they liked the idea of team teaching. We wanted to have a team of mentors that consisted of some who were skilled cooks, others who creatively knew how to set welcoming tables, and several gifted teachers (even if they didn't know it yet). To our amazement, twelve women stepped forward. Who but God would surround us with those who had strengths to complement our weaknesses? Once the team of twelve met to pray and plan, they staged a rebellion and refused to be called wise older women. Hence our program blossomed into Women of Wisdom. We lovingly call this program "mass mentoring," when truthfully it's based on Titus 2. (Note that the focus of Titus 2, and of many of these sessions, is on married women, so if your church has a large proportion of singles, you may have to make an extra effort to make sure single women feel included and that their place in the church is valued.)

Each session addressed one of six subjects. The first was on kindness, which we based on Galatians 5:6, defining kindness as "faith expressing itself through love." We taught the women the importance of speaking kind words and doing kind acts. We advised the ladies of our three Bs:

✤ Not being *blind* to someone else's needs. This involves learning to read between the lines, stand in the gap, and stop being "shoulda, coulda, woulda women." (Refer to chapter 7, Point 2, "Meet Them at Their Needs.")

❧ We explained the *benefits* of kindness. Stressing Matthew 6:1–3, we taught them about anonymous acts of kindness. It's important to understand that God should be glorified, not ourselves. Our pastor had always taught us never to squelch an urge to be generous.

❧ Finally we taught about some *barriers* that can prevent us from doing acts of kindness. Women tend to be too proud of having a full schedule. For example, we turned the word *busy* into an acronym: **B**eing **U**nder **S**atan's **Y**oke. We wanted to illustrate that when in a situation and feeling overwhelmed it's important to ask yourself not, "*How* in the world can I get out of this?" but, "*What* can I get out of this?"

We closed our study of kindness by teaching the young women that every morning they have to get up and get dressed by putting on a heart of compassion, kindness, humility, gentleness, and patience. We had the women come up with a page of random acts of kindness such as: paying the toll for the car behind you, mowing your neighbor's lawn, offering your seat to someone standing on the bus, forgoing a prime parking space, and remembering how your friend likes her coffee and always bringing it to her exactly how she likes it.

The second lesson focused on love for one's husband, which we compared to a fire. We asked each woman to honestly evaluate her marriage. Would she describe it as a flickering flame or a roaring blaze? We covered everything from anger to sex, from forgiveness to the importance of making a commitment to being a praying wife. What better way for a woman to improve her marriage relationship than to pray Psalm 1, Psalm 15, and Psalm 112 each day for her husband? The women learned the importance of speaking life into their husbands by using positive words.

The session devoted to loving one's children was based on Psalm

127:3 (NASB), "Children are a gift of the Lord." We taught about how kids deserve the triple A treatment.

* Affirmation—the importance of speaking life into kids

* Appreciation—all the little ways that a mother can say thanks to her kids just for who they are

* Attention—kids spell love T.I.M.E.

We stressed over and over again the importance of a mother's being with her child 100 percent when she is there. After a crisis kids will remember either their parents' presence or their absence. It's all relative to what a child feels is a crisis: For instance, wetting one's pants in first grade can be just as much a crisis as unexpectedly starting one's period in the sixth grade. We deferred to the wisdom of our pastor's wife as she prepared us for the whole area of discipline. She stressed the proverb "spare the rod and spoil the child." She also drove home the message in 1 Corinthians 15:33: "Bad company corrupts good character."

The fourth lesson was the tough one: submission. God sent us a woman to teach this lesson who is totally committed to submitting to her husband in honor to the Lord. Romance is what all women want to talk about; submission is what most women dread hearing about. Our teacher, who is a forty-five-year-old student at Washington Bible College, had done lengthy research on submission. She simplified it into "yessing and yielding" and openly told the life-changing effects it has had on her marriage.

For the fifth lesson, on purity, we used four teachers to enlighten us. They covered subjects such as the danger of soap operas, addiction to women's magazines and trashy novels, lust, temptations, R-rated movies, gossip, and the horrors of using God's name without reverence and taking God's name in vain. When our children were small and they brought home the phrase "Oh my God" we would tell them they needed to quickly pray because they had now drawn God's attention to them and He was expecting to hear from them. We wove in a lot of material from 1 John 2:15–16: "Do not love the world or anything in the world. If anyone loves the world, the love of the Father is not in him. For everything in the world—the cravings of sinful man, the lust of his eyes and the boasting of what he has and does—comes not from the Father but from the world."

We ended our program by teaching that true hospitality radiates three messages: I care about you, I love you, and I have prepared a place for you. It begins at home with our own families. We need to practice it there first, remembering everyone wears an invisible sign that says "make me feel important." We urged women to strive to have an open home and an open spirit, and concluded by explaining the importance of parading godly people in front of our children. Hospitality can truly be caught as well as taught.

PUTTING TOGETHER THE SESSIONS

Each lesson was created and presented by two women. It proved to be a great way to raise up leaders and mentors, exposing these leaders to the experience of teaching and allowing them to use their spiritual gifts. Paralleling each of the lessons we had a food theme. Appetizers, pasta, poultry, vegetarian dishes, casseroles, and pies were our featured selections. (It was amazing to see how many women had no idea how to debone a chicken, prepare a broth, or make a pie crust from scratch!)

After we had planned our agenda and found our leaders, we needed to find a woman who had a large home and truly loved to entertain. We made the need known and God supplied a volunteer. Our typical evening consisted of opening in prayer, followed by a forty-five-minute cooking demonstration. The simpler and more family oriented the recipes, the more the women seemed to enjoy it. They came away with the feeling of "I can do this." While a few extra ladies cleaned up the kitchen and set the tables, the women being mentored adjourned downstairs to enjoy forty-five minutes of Bible teaching. While they studied the Word, the cooks completed their meal and the table hostesses set elegant tables.

Feast time! The women returned and were seated at each table along with two preselected mentors. While dining, the mentees had the opportunity to ask the mentors any questions pertaining to the day's topic and study.

If you want to mentor, get ready! We live in a real world with real life happenings and challenges. Make yourself open and available to answer any question.

The goal of this entire program is to provide an opportunity for older, wiser women to minister to younger, teachable women based on life experiences. The younger women will learn through each of the studies how important it is to provide a safe place for people, how to serve others (1 Peter 4:8–10), and how to put people before things (Matthew 10:42). Our program was so successful that we now offer it twice a year to new women. We have labeled it W.O.W. 101 and have recently implemented W.O.W. 102. During the second session our topics cover how to have a quiet time, balanced nutrition (Romans 12:1— present your bodies), the attitude of gratitude, right thinking, friendships, and time management. The greatest compliment was given to us during a reunion with the first group of women who had participated in the program. One of the women was telling how W.O.W. had affected her life, and she stated that the program defined womanhood to her. Everyone unanimously agreed!

Five years ago a very wise woman poured her life into us. Carol Anderson, our pastor's wife, dedicated herself to one on one mentoring. The Lord gave us the vision to do this on a larger scale. We realized that we could never pay it back, so we chose to pay it forward! Many definitions make up the word *mentor*. Our women defined it as coming alongside someone, modeling motherhood, teaching, exhorting and encouraging, accountability, and those you are mentoring wanting to grow to be just like you. The Word cites many examples of women mentoring women. Consider Naomi and Ruth, and Elizabeth and Mary. It's a relationship defined by God! After years of unsuccessful mentoring programs, some of our older women felt inadequate or ill equipped or had no time to mentor. Use of our team concept removed these obstacles by sharing the teaching.

In closing, we sought to teach women the importance of being in the company of older and wiser women. Our prayer is that you take the crumbs of our W.O.W. program and create a banquet to suit the needs of the women in your community.

Bobbi Grossmiller has been blessed to be a stay-at-home mom of four while making a "career" of volunteering in her children's schools, their community, and their church. She and Bill, her husband of twenty-five years, live in Bowie, Maryland, with their two youngest children.

Nancy Schrumm, along with her husband, Lew, is currently on staff at Mt. Oak Church as Small Group Coordinator. She and her soul mate Bobbi were instrumental in developing and directing an active and alive women's ministry program. Although a registered nurse by education, her passion is loving and building life into her four children: Amy (now married to Joe with baby Olivia), Tucker, Jeffrey, and Julie. Nancy loves life and lives by Romans 12:11, "Never be lacking in zeal, but keep your spiritual fervor, serving the Lord."

Bobbi and **Nancy** currently lead seminars and workshops training women in leadership positions. It's their desire to see an effective women's ministry firmly planted in every community throughout the country.

FIFTEEN

MENTORING
CHANGES LIVES

Michele Rickett

Standing in the back of the church, looking down the long center aisle, my mind and heart began to race: *I don't see anyone I know. Where should I sit?* It looked like a big party that I was crashing. Any moment I expected someone would notice that I didn't belong and ask me to leave. *This is ridiculous,* I thought; *just find a place to sit down.* As I moved forward it was like the parting of the Red Sea. People looked at me, and looked again. Their stares made me realize just how inappropriately I was dressed for church. I began to tug on the hem of my micro-miniskirt. *Just sit down,* I told myself. *But where?* I didn't want to be too close to the pulpit, I reasoned; the pastor might be able to look inside my soul. I definitely did not want that. So, I found a seat somewhere not too far from the back door.

As I slid into my seat, I gulped. When one sits down wearing a mini-skirt, it disappears. There I was, sitting in church, feeling totally naked! I couldn't wait for the agony to end.

Why would someone like me want to go to church? Simple: I told my new friend that I would go. And I wanted to see this woman again; she had been so kind to me. She invited me to her church, and she said we'd have lunch in her home afterward.

My new friend was the woman I now call mother-in-law, mother-in-love. But at that time, when I was eighteen, she was my boyfriend's mother. Daniel's family was what you might consider ordinary Christians. His dad worked long hours, and his mom was a homemaker and Sunday school teacher, raising four children, dealing with a wayward teenage son. They were wearing their knees out praying for him to come back to Christ. Perhaps he'd meet one of the nice girls in the youth group who would turn his heart back to God. But that was not where his affections came to rest. His affections came to me: the spicy little pagan in a miniskirt. Yet, on the first day his mother laid eyes on me, when she opened the door of her home, she opened the door of her heart. There was not a hint of rejection, just a warm, loving welcome. I was used to rejection. I made a game of that, but this was disarming. This was irresistible.

Mom had everything prepared. The roast had been cooking while we were at church. Homemade bread was being sliced. Pies were steaming on the countertop. The table was set. She wore the "June Cleaver uniform": starched apron over a church dress, accessorized with fake pearl earrings and matching necklace. After our feast Dad read from the biggest Bible I had ever seen, and we prayed. Were these people for real? I was pretty sure it was a show. They couldn't carry on like this all the time . . . could they?

I loved being in their home, so I visited often. I was taking in all the health and goodness of a Christ-centered family. It felt so good to be wanted, loved, and accepted. Daniel's mother talked freely about family and faith. She told me that they had always raised Daniel to surround himself with Christian friends. I blushed. We both knew I wasn't a Christian. But she said that he was old enough to make his own decisions. Daniel saw something special in me, she said, and so did she. She wanted me in her home. I had never been told that I was special, had never felt wanted. There were just two things she requested: that I attend church where they went, and that I have lunch with them afterward. I learned later that this was her secret strategy for me to hear and experience the good news of God's love.

The strategy worked. It was just a matter of time before I wanted the kind of life I saw in this family and the kind of peace, joy, and love I heard from their pastor. After a date one night, Daniel and I prayed for Christ to come into my life, and at that moment my heart was lifted from darkness to light. We immediately ran to tell his mom. Not long after that we married and relocated far from his family, far from the woman who had opened the door of the gospel for me.

When we moved to a new town, I often went to church alone. I still didn't have the wardrobe under control. And it was as if women in the church did not know what to do with someone like me. One woman at church told me that God wanted me to go home and meditate on Proverbs 31. I figured she seemed to know what God wanted, so I went home and searched the whole Bible to find the right page. Reading that passage left me feeling cheated and angry. I felt defeated by the impossible standard of perfection. The little spark of faith in me was almost snuffed out by this woman's good intentions. By contrast, one day I met a Proverbs 31 woman who made the impossible warm, real, and inviting.

One Sunday Anna, an older woman, asked if she could sit with me in church. She introduced herself. She was often alone, she said, a widow raising a daughter. Rather than focusing on her loneliness, she noticed and prayed for others. She noticed me. She wanted to sit together because I was alone too. And in that moment, in her face, I saw the beauty of acceptance and hospitality that I had seen in my mother-in-love. After church Anna invited me to visit her home. We could have lunch and get acquainted. This woman had a secret strategy too.

Through her kitchen-table discipling, Anna planned to teach me every skill that a growing Christian needs to find Christ sufficient. Our textbook was her Bible and concordance. The topics we covered sprang from what she was learning about my needs. Anna didn't have a book or formula to follow. She had a healthy personal faithwalk. She had a Shepherd who led, protected, and nourished her. Over the months of meeting together, I watched her exercise faith in Him. As I began to reveal to Anna how broken I was from growing up without a mother and taking care of a perverse, alcoholic father, she knew what kind of foundation to lay. She led me to wrap my arms around the truth that I have a loving heavenly Father. Anna was an expert builder, teaching me to build a healthy faithwalk. She didn't answer my questions; in wisdom she taught me how to get my questions answered from God's Word. In less than two years with Anna I gained a spiritual skill set and a functioning, growing relationship with Christ that laid a foundation for the rest of my life and ministry.

Now, thirty years later, when I notice a woman alone at church, when I talk with women anywhere—Atlanta, the Middle East, China —or when I sit across my kitchen table from some younger woman, I remember my mentors. I remember the small things that speak indelibly and profoundly: a warm smile and a hug upon meeting, reading a verse before lunch, searching the concordance, praying over problems, sharing a meal at a humble table, showing lovingkindness to the paperboy . . . I've passed on their lessons so many times, even in the remotest places in the world. These things transcend culture and time: Women moved by compassion open their hearts, lives, and homes to other women; they point to and live the truth, always with the expectation that these things are to be passed on to others. My mentors weren't experts or "Bible answer women"; they were co-inquirers of the Lord. Like them, we can work to be master builders—building up the next generation of master builders . . . careful in the way we live, deliberate in teaching these good Titus 2 things to women who will teach others.

Michele Rickett has taken an active leadership role in women's ministries for more than twenty-three years. Michele directs Partners International women's ministry, Sisters In Service. In addition to an international speaking and teaching ministry, Michele has developed numerous workshops and is the author of the Bible study *Ordinary Women: Developing a Faithwalk Worth Passing On.*

PART FOUR

EXPANDING A WOMEN'S MINISTRY

Sometimes the hardest part of any venture is not getting started but staying on target and keeping a clear focus of the purpose God has given you. Sometimes we get frustrated and discouraged with feelings of inadequacy, especially when things don't go exactly as we thought they would. Maybe this story will bring to light God's amazing ability to work all things out for good and to use us, flaws and all, to make this world a better place.

A water bearer in India had two large pots; each pot hung on one end of a pole which the man carried across his neck. One of the pots had a crack in it, while the other pot was perfect. The perfect pot always arrived full at the end of the long walk from the stream to the master's house; the cracked pot arrived only half full.

This daily trek continued for two full years. Of course, the perfect pot was proud of its accomplishments, fulfilling the task it was created for. But the poor cracked pot was ashamed of its flaws, miserable that it fell short of perfection.

One day the flawed pot spoke to the water bearer of its sadness. "I am ashamed of myself, and I want to apologize to you."

"Why?" asked the bearer.

"I have only been able, for the past two years, to carry half my load because this crack in my side causes water to leak out all the way back to your master's house. Because of my flaws, you have to do all of this work, and you don't get the full value for your efforts," the pot said.

The water bearer felt sorry for the old cracked pot, and in his compassion he said, "As we return to the master's house, I want you to notice the beautiful flowers along the path."

Indeed, as they went up the hill, the old cracked pot took notice of the sun warming the beautiful wildflowers on the side of the path, and this cheered it some. But at the end of the trail, it still felt the pang of sadness, because it had leaked out half its load, and so again it apologized to the bearer for its failure.

Then the bearer asked, "Did you notice that there were flowers only on your side of the path, but not on the other pot's side?" The pot nodded.

"That's because I have always known about your flaw, and I took advantage of it. I planted flower seeds on your side of the path, and every day while we walked back from the stream, you've watered them. For two years I have been able to pick these beautiful flowers to decorate my master's table. If you were not created thus, my master would not have had this beauty grace his house."[1]

May this encourage your heart as we journey deeper into the building of a women's ministry. You may not feel adequate or able, but through you God can plant seeds of hope and love in women's hearts. Then your Master will rejoice in the beautiful bouquets that come from your efforts.

So many women need to be reached with the love of Jesus—women inside and outside the walls of our churches. I encourage you to expand your vision and reach out arms of love to touch all the women God brings into your sphere of influence.

---

[1] Ann Fox Chodakowski and Susan Fox Wood, *Moms Saving Money* (Eugene, Ore.: Harvest House, 2000), 218–19.

SIXTEEN

THINKING OUTSIDE THE BOX TO REACH WOMEN

Chris Adams

Sarah is a new mom who feels very overwhelmed and stressed-out from the constant demands of her little one and of trying to manage her home. Diane is a career woman who is frustrated with her husband and ready to call it quits on her six-year marriage. Patty is a beautiful woman envied by all her friends, but behind the perfect figure and gorgeous smile is a painful past that haunts her and makes her feel worthless. Georgia is a stay-at-home mother of three who feels very sure in her calling to be at home with her kids but also struggles with feelings of frustration and anger. Different women on different paths have a common thread woven into their lives—they need Jesus and encouragement from other godly women who will constantly and lovingly point them to Him.

Every ministry of the church today is vital, and women's ministry is certainly no exception. Women have unique needs and struggles with which only other women can really identify. There are so many women who come to church who may be saved but that's as far as it goes. Women's ministries can help disciple such a woman and prepare her to move into ministry and service. Just as our churches are different, women's ministries too come in all shapes and sizes. We must make room for growth until our women's ministries expand to include every woman who needs to be ministered to and every woman who needs to minister. We need not be afraid to think outside the box to minister in unique ways that can reach the women God has entrusted to us.

OUT OF THE SIGN-UP-SHEET BOX

Serving in a church is not an option—it is our responsibility. However, we need to use caution when moving women into service. It is vitally important to teach women how to *be,* not just to *do* all the time. One of the number one issues that needs to be addressed in women's ministries today is stress and balance. Women have so much to do already, and sometimes churches make this problem worse. Discipling a woman to have a close personal relationship with the Lord and helping her grow in her ability to hear and discern His will is most important. Then she can hear God's calling and be sure of what she is to do and how she is to use the gifts He's given to her.

We must shift our thinking from passing out sign-up sheets and requiring women to serve because the need is there to letting their service grow out of a place where their lives have been touched. Today women are busy. But even busy women are willing to participate and contribute to activities that make a difference in their lives and in the lives of others. The most dedicated ministry servers you'll find most often grew out of the most deeply touched ministry receivers.

OUT OF THE ACTIVITIES BOX

When thinking about the future of your women's ministry, ask yourself these questions, "Why do we exist?" "Why does this ministry exist?" and, "Where do I want to see these women in ten years?" After answering these questions, convey the vision God gives you to the women involved. Instead of just planning for this year and plugging things into the calendar, plan for the years to come. Plan for transformed lives.

Too many times we get stuck in a rut of doing activity for activity's sake and forget that women are really looking for deep spiritual content in those activities. We need to get intentional with our ministries, events, and studies. Talk to your ladies about key issues they want to see addressed. You may even survey women outside the walls of your church and find out what topics interest them. Make a list of key issues and pray God would give you wisdom in knowing how to address these. Always make it a top priority to clearly weave the gospel into all areas of your women's ministry.

OUT OF THE ASSUMPTION BOX

Too many of us assume that programs equal ministry. Although purposeful programs and events are important, our first commitment must be to ministry. Terry Hershey identifies the differences between programs and ministry:

* Programs focus on techniques—ministry focuses on people.

* Programs look for numbers—ministry sees changed lives.

* Programs need quick answers—ministry understands grace in uncertainty.

* Programs see the course—ministry sees the hearts.[1]

People, changed lives, grace, and hearts drawn to God are what it's all about. Remember what Jesus said in Matthew 22:37–39 when asked which is the greatest commandment. "Jesus replied, 'Love the Lord your God with all your heart and with all your soul and with all your mind.' This is the first and greatest commandment. And the second is like it: 'Love your neighbor as yourself.'" That's what matters most of all.

OUT OF THE BUDGET BOX

If your church budget does not include monies for women's ministry this year, find out when the budget will be set for the next year and make a proposal to be included. When there is no budget, you can get creative. Here are just a few suggestions:

* Each event or activity must recover its cost by selling tickets and workbooks/materials and charging for child care.

* Decorations can be handmade or purchased and resold at the event. Women are usually willing to bring items from home or donate them.

* When conducting Bible studies that require the purchase of leader books, leader kits, and workbooks, each woman should purchase her own workbook as an investment in her own spiritual growth. Additionally, group members could be charged a few extra dollars to cover the cost of leader materials.

* Two smaller churches may join together to purchase the materials, then stagger their starting dates by a couple of weeks so both can use the resources.

* For special events, make the needs known to the church. Many in your church have the gift of giving and the means to do so. If they know about the needs they will gladly contribute money,

time, or other resources to help with your ministry activities and special events.[2]

Now back to Sarah, Diane, Patty, and Georgia. These women are like thousands of women in neighborhoods and churches across America. They need Jesus. They need godly women to disciple and mentor them. They need to be surrounded by love and care from those in a women's ministry. They need a women's ministry director who isn't afraid to think outside the box and reach them with life-changing ministry.

Chris Adams has served as Women's Enrichment Ministry/Ministers' Wives Specialist for LifeWay Church Resources since 1994. She has compiled two women's ministry leadership books, *Women Reaching Women: Beginning and Building a Growing Women's Enrichment Ministry* and *Transformed Lives: Taking Women's Ministry to the Next Level.* Chris has a passion to assist churches in beginning and developing effective ministry to and with women, as well as reaching and discipling women for Christ. She is married to Pat and has grown twin daughters and four grandchildren.

---

[1] Terry Hershey, *Young Adult Ministry* (Loveland, Colo.: Group, 1986), 70.
[2] Chris Adams, *Transformed Lives* (Nashville: LifeWay Press, 1999), 214.

SEVENTEEN

REACHING THE NEXT GENERATION ONE WOMAN AT A TIME

Cheri Jimenez

"One generation shall praise Your works to another, and shall declare Your mighty acts."

∽PSALM 145:4 NASB

What if Jesus had walked alone? What if there were no Matthew, Peter, James, and John? Who would have written the story of Jesus, and who would have led His church? What if Jesus had simply passed them by and not asked them to follow Him?

It is through the life of Jesus that we see how important it is to invest in the next generation on a personal level. Jesus shared the depth of His commitment to do the will of the Father with those around Him. His sacrificial investment into the next generation was poured into the lives of a select group of potential leaders. And His leadership style always made lasting impressions. Jesus begins to invest in the lives of others by sending out *personal* invitations, giving *personal* instruction, and leading others with His own *personal* influence.

I believe that influencing the next generation—those young women who will someday assume positions of leadership—is one of the most essential facets of women's ministry. This concept of leadership investment was extended to me as a young woman, and it is my desire to build this legacy among the next generation of leaders. In preparing young women for leadership, we have the profound opportunity to influence generation after generation. This multiplying effect of leadership has the potential to radically change the landscape of Christian ministry.

The Scriptures are filled with powerful examples of influencing the next generation by investing in leadership. In Deuteronomy 31, Moses prepared Joshua to lead the Israelites to the Promised Land. The apostle Paul intentionally invested in young Timothy when he was charged to carry on their work: "And the things you have heard me say in the presence of many witnesses entrust to reliable men who will also be qualified to teach others" (2 Timothy 2:2).

Just as Moses found Joshua in the local camp and Paul found young Timothy in the idolatrous city of Lystra, so we are called to search out leaders in all walks of life. Have you thought about the young women in your local church or community who will someday be leaders? What about those you have met in the workplace or ministry outlets? What do you know about their personal lives and the struggles inherent within to their generation?

An important component of leadership investment includes a study of the culture and the individuals you intend to reach. Understanding the culture will provide you with vital information to expand and enhance your scope of influence. Let's take a brief look at the background from which our future leaders are emerging.

Labeled by the media and pop culture as Generations X, Y, and Z, this upcoming group of young people are seeking refuge and refreshment at local churches in record numbers, according to the Barna Research Group. Unlike any other generational group in recent history, younger women are searching for meaning and hope to counterbalance the often confusing and contradictory images of society. Many of their attitudes and belief systems have been shaped and shattered by the failed philosophies of feminism. This generation has grown up with Oprah as a spiritual mentor and *Cosmopolitan* as an image consultant. Truth has been mixed with error, and statistics consistently confirm that this generation tends to be apathetic toward absolute moral standards. However, in desperation, they seek for a cause they can believe in and identity with to bring significance and purpose to life. These cultural trends present numerous opportunities to expose the next generation to the transforming truth of God's Word. The church will have a vast and fertile population for discipleship and leadership training.

In this chapter, we will examine how Jesus modeled leadership investment. In fact, His entire leadership style during His three years of ministry was to invite, instruct, and influence others for the furtherance of the gospel. Jesus accepted individuals as they were, taught them the truth, and kept them accountable. Using this method, and of course relying on the Holy Spirit's power, Jesus graduated exceptional leaders, the apostles, who inaugurated His church. Their influence spread Christianity into a worldwide movement. Let's practically explore these three points of leadership investment.

THE OPPORTUNITY TO INVITE

"Good leaders have a vision, better leaders share a vision; the best leaders invite others to join them in spreading this vision."
∞BOB BRINER AND RAY PRITCHARD

Jesus extended personal invitations. He called all of His disciples using this approach. And don't you just love the motley crew He invited to be His message bearers? In calling Matthew, a despised tax collector, Jesus went against conventional wisdom and looked far beneath the surface. In doing so, He demonstrated an important leadership lesson. Jesus recognized what the Holy Spirit could accomplish through Matthew. He envisioned Matthew as he was to become, a future leader and one of His biographers. Jesus clearly understood that obatacles could indeed be turned into opportunities. Jesus invited Matthew to follow Him, and we get the privilege of witnessing his lifestyle transformation throughout the Gospels.

Discerning whom to invite is often a challenge. As humans, we do not possess the Savior's power of omniscience. But the good news is He has given His Spirit to guide us. Psalm 32:8 (NASB) tells us that God will guide us with His eye. Through His power, we are able to invite as He did. We are also reminded in Proverbs 4:7–8 that wisdom from God is the principal thing, and therefore we must be willing to embrace and submit to it daily. This will give us the confidence and certainty required to extend a personal invitation.

I encourage you to start praying now for God to lay on your heart and bring across your path those who need to be invited into leadership. Remember to start looking for every opportunity to make a leadership investment. Prayer and the Word of God are essential to this process. You will stand amazed at the faithfulness of God as He leads you to those who are ripe for leadership training. Those you invite will also be eternally grateful for your act of investment. In your quiet time, ask God to start implanting the following characteristics in the young women:

* A Humble Heart

* A Teachable Heart

* A Servant's Heart

Remember that God can use anyone, talented or not, who possesses these character qualities. Trust the Holy Spirit to help you, *personally* and intentionally, to reach out to the next generation in love and acceptance. They are looking for servant leadership in action. Jesus invited people to follow Him, and so should we. Send someone a *personal* invitation. This is what leadership is all about.

INSPIRED TO INVEST

Practical Suggestions to Implement the Principle of Inviting

Personally invite a high school, college, or young single woman to be a part of a leadership council (a select group of women who assist the director to carry out ministry objectives). This act of invitation helps join together women of different ages and stages of life.

Using this setting, observe these young women interacting with other leaders and responding to leadership opportunities. Do they exhibit humility? Are they teachable? Are they willing to serve where needed?

Be willing to use their input and suggestions. It will help to better meet the spiritual and social needs of this generation. Their ideas will be creative and allow you to think outside the box.

When opportunity allows, spend one-on-one time with these young women. Listen to them; share their burdens, joys, questions, and struggles. Pray with them, encourage them, and befriend them!

THE OPPORTUNITY TO INSTRUCT

"It is interesting that of all the ways Paul could have told the women to combat the decadence of their culture, he told them to invest their energies in teaching their younger women to live Christianly in their society."

∽SUSAN HUNT

Jesus fulfilled many roles in His ministry, but those closest to Him lovingly referred to Him as teacher. He could turn any place into a classroom, and He used every conceivable setting to teach His disciples. Whether on the seashore or in the synagogue, He allowed time for instruction. Jesus was an effective teacher because He taught by both precept and example. This made His instruction purposeful and powerful.

Scripture tells us that Jesus spoke to the masses but taught His disciples. Individual time is where Jesus deposited His truths in a more intimate way. He poured His life into a few, and they impacted the world and all of history. It is a leader's responsibility to impart insight and inspiration into a concentrated group. In doing so, the leadership cycle has the capacity to have significant long-term results. Consider the remarkable results Jesus' disciples achieved after His departure through the power of the Holy Spirit.

Many of the young women coming into congregations today have not grown up in the church. These young women often lack solid foundations in areas of doctrine and theology. And they need to be taught. By encouraging the next generation toward spiritual maturity, we actually enable them to realize their purpose and use their gifts. This process of instruction builds their confidence and inspires them to a greater vision of what their future ministry might be.

So what should we teach the next generation of leaders? In 2 Timothy 3:16–17, we read that all Scripture is profitable for doctrine, for reproof, for correction, for instruction in righteousness, so that we might grow to maturity. Here are some foundational components of instruction for young women in the church and ministry.

1. *Counsel of Doctrine*—What God's Word teaches about foundations of faith

2. *Commitment to Character*—What God's Word teaches about spiritual maturity

3. *Celebration of Purpose*—What God's Word teaches about embracing God's unique calling as women

4. *Contentment of Life*—What God's Word teaches about stages and seasons of women's lives

5. *Command to Influence*—What God's Word teaches about using your gifts and talents for service

6. *Challenge to Ministry*—What God's Word teaches about leadership and passing on a spiritual legacy

The Bible offers explicit guidelines of instruction for leadership investment. In the book of Titus, Paul instructs Titus by writing him a letter to assist others in leadership training. In Titus 2:7–8, Paul reminds Titus how imperative his own personal conduct and example is to ensure the success of his leadership investment in others. As Christian leaders, our instruction must correlate into how we live. When we "practice what we preach," it gives credibility to our message. Instruction must be transparent and authentic to last. Jesus' vision was contagious because He allowed others to see Him up close.

INSPIRED TO INVEST

Practical Suggestions to Implement the Principle of Instruction

Implement a leaders' accountability group. Surround yourself with other godly leaders who can continue to sharpen your spiritual growth and potential as a leader. Make yourself accountable *to them!*

Set personal goals to study God's Word through your own devotions, Scripture memory, prayer, and fasting. Ask God for special insight and inspiration to pass on.

Lead an accountability group for younger leaders. Allow time for one-on-one instruction to provide biblical teaching on subjects and issues that need to be addressed.

Allow young leaders to ask questions about your life experience. Be honest and vulnerable with them—they will be honored you trust them with this information.

THE OPPORTUNITY TO INFLUENCE

"Great influencers know how to nurture the potential in others to fulfill their God-given purpose."

∞CAROL KENT

Jesus calls us to be influential in the lives of those in whom we invest. As I speak across the country, I am frequently asked how to influence and connect with the next generation—a generation shy of commitment and leery of truth. While these characteristics often present challenges in ministering to them, time and energy still remain key ingredients of influence. There are no shortcuts. There are no formulas. Jesus sacrificially gave of Himself to train and prepare His followers.

I believe that in showing this generation that we are willing to invest ourselves and speak the truth, we earn the opportunity to influence women one at a time. Jesus spent time investing into His disciples, and there is no substitute. Jesus ate with the disciples, He traveled with them, and, in the confines of a small group, He explained His stories, miracles, and parables. It took time. It required commitment. Jesus' example of influence has stood the test of time and has affected the world for centuries. Jesus demonstrated several noteworthy characteristics that made His influence so revolutionary.

1. Jesus was an Encourager—*He recognized one's full potential.*

2. Jesus was an Equipper—*He nurtured one's God-given purpose.*

3. Jesus was an Exhorter—*He identified one's possible pitfalls.*

I love the story of the impetuous disciple, Peter. Many may have considered investing in him to be a great risk. Peter often spoke without thinking and acted on his feelings, and the Bible tells us that he denied Christ three times. But Jesus did not give up on Peter. Jesus encouraged, equipped, and exhorted Peter throughout His three years of ministry. Jesus believed in Peter and reminded him that failure was not final. And when the time came for Peter to finally assume the reins of leadership, he was ready. Despite Peter's mistakes, God used him to preach at Pentecost and bring thousands to salvation in Christ. Jesus saw Peter's potential to lead others to the heart of God. This too is our mission!

As a way of personal testimony, I would like to say how I have been influenced by intentional investment. Mrs. Beverly LaHaye, Founder and President of Concerned Women for America (CWA), clearly understood the importance of developing leaders to transform society. When I was a young intern at CWA, Mrs. LaHaye invited me to share her vision while giving me opportunities to develop as a leader. She took time to instruct me. Her vast experiences and life's lessons served as learning tools that shaped my expectations and vision for future ministry.

I have to admit that Mrs. LaHaye took a big risk when she promoted me to a leadership position. Although I was not the top candidate for the job, she trusted in what God would do with my life. My years at CWA proved to be invaluable as I sat at the feet of someone I greatly loved and admired. I thank the Lord that Mrs. LaHaye took the time and energy to invest in a young, impressionable woman. In training young leaders, she in essence has impacted women around the globe. This is the multiplication theory at work!

Mrs. LaHaye's investment has inspired me to invest in others the same way. As a result of her involvement in my life, she has affected my own generation every time I influence others. This notable Christian leader not only preserved but also multiplied the truth of the gospel by making a personal investment in me. To transfer this type of influence is what links one generation to the next. Simply put, this is how one begins the process of reaching the next generation—leading women to the heart of God one woman at a time.

INSPIRED TO INVEST

Practical Suggestions to Implement the Principle of Influence

Think about the individuals who influenced your life as a leader. How did they encourage, equip, and exhort you? Start praying that God will give you opportunities to extend the same type of influence.

Commit to following current events to sustain an accurate knowledge of the negative influences that affect the next generation. Gather resources and materials to help you connect and relate to their generation. You cannot influence if you are out of touch.

Engage yourself in the next generation. Search for common interests and values you may have with potential leaders. Use these as avenues to develop relationships.

Spend time with young leaders. Ask questions. Seek to find out what the next generation thinks, feels, and needs most in life. What are their fears, dreams, and aspirations?

Cheri Jimenez is influencing her home as a wife and mother. She is the President of the Embracing Womanhood Project, a ministry dedicated to reaching young women and training leaders on issues of biblical womanhood. Previously, Cheri served as the Executive Director of The Proverbs 31 Ministry, Communications Director for the North Carolina Family Policy Council, and Director of Broadcasting and Media for Concerned Women for America (CWA). Cheri graduated with a B.A. in Public Speaking with graduate work in Communications and Organizational Leadership. She also serves as Women's Ministry Director at Providence Baptist Church in Raleigh, North Carolina.

EIGHTEEN

TIME TO REACH OUT— CHURCH AND THE SINGLE WOMAN

Michelle McKinney Hammond

As the rising number of singles sends shock waves through the church community, a resounding question rises to the forefront: "What should we be doing with the singles?" No one seems to know. Those who are married are relieved they don't have to deal with the challenges of loneliness and uncertain tomorrows, yet they don't have the time or resources to know how to minister to the singles effectively. In the flurry of misunderstanding, the church fails to tap into two incredible resources that the single woman embodies: availability to serve and passion.

Unfortunately, far too often, the general perception of the single is one of inconsistency and unreliability. The fact that many of these women are effective professionals in their given field is overlooked. It is like going off to the mines every day in search of diamonds never realizing there are gems in your own backyard.

Yet Paul blatantly summed up the fact that singleness is a gift, not just to the *individual* but to the *church,* by writing,

> But a married man is concerned about the affairs of this world—how he can please his wife—and his interests are divided. An unmarried woman or virgin is concerned about the Lord's affairs: Her aim is to be devoted to the Lord in both body and spirit. But a married woman is concerned about the affairs of this world—how she can please her husband. (1 Corinthians 7:33–34)

Well! Paul said a mouthful! When we take a look at Scripture, we see many women following and serving Jesus. I can most assuredly say that those women who followed Jesus and served the disciples were single. Jesus stated, "Who are my mother and my brothers," in order to qualify that we are now all part of a great kingdom family, and this statement has led some to believe that Jesus was suggesting that family should take a backseat to their "calling." Not true! I can stand on the Rock and say this with confidence: I doubt very seriously that He ever looked a married woman in the eye and said, "Leave your husband and children and follow Me."

Jesus took marriage as seriously as the Father did. To married women I believe He said, "Stand with your husband and your family and establish My kingdom where you are in partnership with your loved ones." Deborah, a judge in Israel, was a fine of example of this. After all, it is listed that she was the wife of Lappidoth, something God did not overlook, which leads me to believe that she fulfilled this role as well. Though she was judge of Israel, the way she handled her position led the nation of Israel to call her a "mother of Israel." She did not insist on charging into battle but left room for the men around her to fulfill their roles. There were also New Testament women like Priscilla, who, along with her husband, held church in her home. But to the singles who were available, with no ties to hinder their movement or divide their time, Jesus said, "You can physically and actively follow Me." Some hit the road with Him, and others worked in their communities to effect change for the kingdom.

Single women who stand out in Scripture as effecting significant changes in biblical history include Rahab, who hid the spies from Israel, thus enabling the Israelites to infiltrate enemy territory and conquer Jericho; Ruth, the Moabitess, who walked her mother-in-law Naomi back to Bethlehem in Judah, married Boaz, and bore a son who would be included in the lineage of Christ; the woman at the well, who ended up evangelizing Samaria; Mary, who bore Jesus; Mary Magdalene, who was the first to see and announce that Jesus had risen. These were women who were sensitive to the leading of God. Though some eventually were married, they were chosen as single women to fit into God's divine plan.

Now I just heard someone say, "Some lineup that was: One was a harlot, one was an idol worshiper, one was an adulteress, and the other one had to have seven demons cast out of her!" Ah, and you are so right. But what is the common thread with all of these women? I'll tell you. Passion. That's right. Passion.

You've heard the phrase "An idle mind is the devil's workshop." Indeed it is. Passion is the seat from which worship reigns. Small wonder the devil would take advantage of an empty seat and set up shop to pervert our passions and misdirect our worship. If singles are not totally saturated with a passion for carrying out the purposes of God, believe me the devil will find plenty for them to do. God knew who to choose for jobs that required risk and boldness. He found women like Rahab, Ruth, and the rest of the above-mentioned prime candidates to accomplish His mission on earth.

Why? Not only because they were available for the task but because they were women who were sold out to whatever they felt strongly about. In spite of their past He extended His grace to them and redirected their passions to fulfill God's purposes.

THE CHURCH AND SINGLES

So what is the church's responsibility toward singles? First, to include singles as full, profitable members of the church rather than people on the sidelines you forget about. Second, the church is called to cover these women. Dinah, the daughter of Jacob, and Tamar, the daughter of King David, were both single women who were raped by unbelievers. In the natural we consider that to be a physical violation, but in the spirit a deeper spiritual principle was at work—it is an emotional and spiritual violation. When we fail to cover single women in our church community, they are open to anything (the wrong men and nonvictorious relationships) and left defenseless when the Enemy assaults them. The church needs to surround these women and be responsible for their emotional and physical safety. How? By feeding their spirits with sound direction and providing them with a strong sense of community that builds them up in their sense of worth and purpose and lessens their feelings of being alone or isolated.

Providing literal help for single parents is certainly an overlooked duty that churches have. In far too many churches, no thought is given to meaningful activities or programs that feed and strengthen singles overall. Conferences for married people abound with incredible speakers and seminars, yet the crumbs of social activities are thrown to singles, as if all they want to do is have a place to meet a mate. What about giving singles more meaning in life? Making them feel as if they are a necessary and vital part of the body of Christ? How about directing their passions away from themselves and their single state and back toward the service of God? Now we're talking.

SINGLES ON A MISSION

There is nothing more glorious to behold than singles with a purpose, singles on a mission for God. It is time to redirect the focus of singles and equip them to be whole and productive. Single women have the incredible opportunity to fulfill the purpose of motherhood in the kingdom. What do I mean by that? Like Mary, we are all called, as believers, to bear Christ to the world! When we know God, we become living epistles representing Christ in the earth, thus birthing others into the kingdom. To have a baby is a function, but to be a mother is to fulfill a purpose. When single women couple their knowledge of God with their passion for using their gifts and abilities for His purposes, they too are fruitful and able to multiply. Multiply babies, unbelievers, into the kingdom of God. Nurse those who are babies in the body until they are able to eat strong meat. Serve strong meat and equip others for the effectual work of the ministry.

The cycle of productivity can be astounding when singles step into their God-given assignments. Small wonder Isaiah proclaimed,

> "Sing, O barren woman, you who never bore a child; burst into song, shout for joy, you who were never in labor; because more are the children of the desolate woman than of her who has a husband," says the Lord. "Enlarge the place of your tent, stretch your tent curtains wide, do not hold back; lengthen your cords, strengthen your stakes. For you will spread out to the right and to the left; your descendants will dispossess nations and settle in their desolate cities. Do not be afraid; you will not suffer shame. Do not fear disgrace; you will not be humiliated. You will forget the shame of your youth and remember no more the reproach of your widowhood. For your Maker is your husband—the Lord Almighty is his name—the Holy One of Israel is your Redeemer; he is called the God of all the earth." (Isaiah 54:1–5)

Perhaps the biological clocks of single women are ticking for a reason. Though many long for physical babies, perhaps there is a greater purpose behind this deep desire that cannot be shaken. Perhaps singles are in travail because the church is not giving them the opportunity to labor for the kingdom. It is not mates or children that are the primary need for the single women; it is the fulfillment of their God-ordained purpose. It is the responsibility and obligation of every church, like the Good Shepherd to lead their singles to nourishing pasture where provision is made to nourish and sustain this very important part of the body. All of us are necessary to the body's health:

> Now the body is not made up of one part but of many. If the foot should say, "Because I am not a hand, I do not belong to the body," it would not for that reason cease to be part of the body. And if the ear should say, "Because I am not an eye, I do not belong to the body," it would not for that reason cease to be part of the body. If the whole body were an eye, where would the sense of hearing be? If the whole body were an ear, where would the sense of smell be? But in fact God has arranged the parts in the body, every one of them, just as he wanted them to be. If they were all one part, where would the body be? As it is, there are many parts, but one body.
>
> The eye cannot say to the hand, "I don't need you!" And the head cannot say to the feet, "I don't need you!" On the contrary, those parts of the body that seem to be weaker are indispensable, and the parts that we think are less honorable we treat with special honor. And the parts that are unpresentable are treated with special modesty, while our presentable parts need no special treatment. But God has combined the members of the body and has given greater honor to the parts that lacked it, so that there should be no division in the body, but that its parts should have equal concern for each other. If one part suffers, every part suffers with it; if one part is honored, every part rejoices with it.
>
> Now you are the body of Christ, and each one of you is a part of it. (1 Corinthians 12:14–27)

If that isn't food for thought, I don't know what is.

Michelle McKinney Hammond is a speaker and singer at women's conferences, universities, and churches. She is also a cohost of the Emmy-award nominated show *Aspiring Women*. As the Founder and President of HeartWing Ministries, she dedicates full-time service to writing and speaking, inspiring Christians to return to the basics of a love-driven relationship with God. She is also the author of more than twelve books including *How to Be Blessed and Highly Favored*.

NINETEEN

REACHING OUT TO THE COMMUNITY WITH LIFESTYLE EVANGELISM

Renee Swope

Our neighborhoods, workplaces, and communities are filled with women looking for meaning, searching for unfailing love, and striving toward fulfillment. Many have given up on God and the church. What they need is a friend. They need someone who will open her heart and share her life in a way that allows them to see Jesus through her lifestyle.

As we reach out to our communities, it is important that we seek to live a lifestyle of evangelism. When you hear the word *evangelism,* what picture comes to your mind? Do you see Billy Graham speaking in front of thousands of people? Some of us picture a preacher on the street corner shaking his Bible and shouting John 3:16 as people pass by. Others see a pair of churchgoers wearing their Sunday best visiting door-to-door in neighborhoods.

Although each of these may be a form of evangelism, the mere thought of doing them makes most of us want to run in the opposite direction. Why is it that evangelism paints in our minds pictures that just don't fit in to the scenery of our lives? Perhaps it's because we've never seen it lived out any other way. As we look at what it means to live a lifestyle of evangelism, I hope to paint in your mind a picture that makes you want to live it, not run from it.

According to Webster, evangelism is *a zealous effort to spread the gospel,* and lifestyle is *an integrated way of life.*[1] The goal of lifestyle evangelism is to spread the gospel with zealous efforts as an integrated way of life. Let's break it down and look at the meaning of four key words.

Zealous: ardently (strongly) devoted to a purpose

Effort: a conscious attempt to achieve a particular end

Spread: open or stretch out to cover more space; unfold; to lay in display; to cause to be more widely known

Gospel: the teachings of Jesus and the apostles; the belief in man's redemption through Jesus as Christ

A LIFESTYLE OF EVANGELISM

Living a lifestyle of evangelism means we make a conscious attempt to unfold the gospel and lay on display the truths of Christ in relationships we have with people who don't know Him. The life and teachings of Jesus become such an integrated way of living that He becomes more widely known among those who know us.

Sharing my faith became a core value early on in my life as a Christian. Soon after surrendering to Christ at the age of twenty-two, I joined a church that strongly emphasized evangelism. The people-pleaser in me assumed my spiritual maturity and my value in the church would increase based on how many people I explained the gospel to.

Perhaps God would be more pleased and others would think more highly of me. Maybe that degree in marketing I had just received led me to think I'd get a bigger bonus in heaven and in my church if I brought in more customers.

Although my motives were wrong, God used my efforts and several people accepted Christ. However, people became projects, and trying to impress God and others left me feeling empty and confused. It has been thirteen years, and I've learned a lot since then. No longer do I discuss my faith out of obligation. Telling others about Christ is more like sharing a gift that is too good to keep all to myself.

THE ABC'S OF LIFESTYLE EVANGELISM

Abiding in Christ

To abide means *to stay, to reside with.* Jesus chose the Twelve to be His disciples, for the purpose that they "might be with him" (Mark 3:14). He'd eventually send them out to "preach and to have authority to drive out demons" (v. 15), but Jesus made clear that before these men were to do ministry, they were to be "with Him." Often we overlook what came first.

Luke 8:10 tells us that by simply being with Him, the disciples were given "the knowledge of the secrets of the kingdom of God." Often we don't talk about our faith because we feel inadequate or afraid we won't know what to say. We think, *If I just had more faith.*

Author John Ortberg says, "Never try to have more faith, just get to know God better. And because God is faithful, the better you know Him, the more you'll trust Him."[2] How do we get to know God better? By spending time with Him and reading His Word.

Not only do we gain faith when we get to know God better, but the aroma of Christ begins to permeate our lives. Second Corinthians 2:15 says, "We are to God the aroma of Christ among those who are being saved." It reminds me of my dating days when I would snuggle with my boyfriend on the couch for hours. After he went home I'd scrunch my shirt close to my face and breathe in the scent of him. Although he was gone, the smell of his cologne reminded me of him. The same is true when we spend time abiding in Christ. It produces such a strong concentration of His influence in our lives that His power and presence will be undeniable to others.

Here are several ways we can *abide* in Christ:

* Reading and feeding on the truths of the Bible

* Communicating with God in prayer (listening and talking)

* Spending time with other Christians; encouraging and spurring each other on

* Worshiping Him in music

* Serving in church as a part of the body of Christ

* Actively telling others about our faith

To abide also means *to remain.* It is essential that we remain in Christ as we live a lifestyle of evangelism. In His last conversation with the disciples before He was arrested, Jesus told them how important it would be that they remain in Him. "Abide in Me, and I in you," He said. "As the branch cannot bear fruit of itself unless it abides in the vine, so neither can you unless you abide in Me. I am the vine, you are the branches; he who abides in Me and I in him, he bears much fruit, for apart from Me you can do nothing" (John 15:4–5 NASB).

Building Relationships with Nonbelievers

Jesus said the greatest commandment is to "'love the Lord your God with all your heart and with all your soul and with all your mind.

. . . The second is like it: 'Love your neighbor as yourself.'"

The first part, loving God, comes when we abide. The second part, loving our neighbor, is a natural overflow of the first. From the beginning of time, God has been in relationship. John 1:1 tells us that Jesus was always with God, but They didn't form a clique and close the doors. They invited others in, and He wants us to do so as well.

Just as Jesus told His disciples to give as freely as they had received (Matthew 10:8) and to love one another as He loved them (John 13:34–35), we are told to give our lives away. As they had seen for three years, the disciples were to give themselves in selfless devotion to those whom the Father loved and for whom Jesus would die (John 17:23).

For others to see that kind of love as they watch our lives, our attitudes, and our relationships, they will need to be close enough to look in. It is tempting to build a wall around our lives to protect our family and ourselves from the world. But when God said to let our light "shine among men," He didn't mean within the walls of our churches or in the homes of our Christian friends. The Light is already shining there. He wants us to take our light out into the darkness by building relationships with nonbelievers.

People will know we are Jesus' disciples by the way we love each other and the way we love them. This past year my husband and I were faced with a difficult situation that gave us the opportunity to apply this principle. My next door neighbor Paul,* a fifty-one-year-old man, committed suicide. It was one of the most devastating experiences of my life. However, what it did to me was nothing compared to the wake of despair it left behind. When he abandoned this life on earth, he also abandoned a very lonely seventy-five-year-old mother who lived with him.

Paul called the police to tell them his plans and asked them to come get his mother. Amelia,* Paul's mother, was taken out safely, but the

---

*Names changed for privacy.

193

police did not go in. Concerned that he might come out shooting, the sheriff's department brought in a whole army of officers. A S.W.A.T. team surrounded my home, and we were unable to leave for hours.

It was eleven o'clock that Tuesday night when the police finally broke into his home, but it was too late. We were exhausted and needed to go to bed. Scheduled to leave for Chicago on Thursday, I knew we'd be taking on an overwhelming responsibility if we got involved. Why not just shut my door and let the police handle it? The easiest thing would be to bring the mother a card, cook her a meal, and pray for her.

Then the question crossed my mind: What would Jesus do? I know He'd walk right into the crisis. He would hold Amelia and comfort her. Once the police said we could come out of our home, I walked out the door, asked the police if she needed a place to stay while the investigators finished their work, and offered for them to bring her to our home. Along with a police officer and the chaplain, she came and stayed until 3:00 A.M.

In the midst of tragedy God invited us to be Jesus with skin on. He also gave us an eyewitness view of lifestyle evangelism. The officer assigned to the case had lost her own mother to suicide, she was a Christian, and she told Amelia the story of hope she had found in her relationship with Jesus. Bill Fogarty, senior pastor of a local church, was the chaplain called in for Amelia. He volunteers his "free time" to bring Light into the dark places of our city. He prayed with her and assured her that Jesus cared and that He'd be there for her. The next day Bill returned to listen and help guide her through funeral arrangements.

Months have passed. Amelia has come to church with us and attended women's dinners where an evangelistic message was presented. We have prayed with her, discussed the gospel with her one-on-one, and done our best to bring His light into her darkness. God has taken something tragic and worked it for her good. The neighbors have joined hearts and hands to love her. Five families take turns making sure she has groceries, transportation, visits, opportunities to go to church, and friends like she never had before. We represent three denominations, and the love of Christ is being displayed in each of us.

Communicating Christ in Everyday Life

As we abide in Christ and build relationships with unbelievers, we need to learn how to effectively communicate Christ to others. The greatest tool we have to communicate Christ is the Holy Spirit. By relying on the Holy Spirit for wisdom and discernment, we are able to recognize His timing and speak the appropriate words. In the days that followed my neighbor's death, the Holy Spirit guided us and ministered through us as we depended on Him.

In *The Master Plan of Evangelism,* Robert Coleman reminds us:

> It is only the Spirit of God who enables us to carry on the redemptive mission of evangelism. Jesus underscored this early in His ministry by declaring that what He did was in cooperation with the Spirit of the Lord. We read in Isaiah 61:1 that it was by the anointing of the Spirit that he preached the gospel to the poor, healed the broken hearted, proclaimed deliverance to the captive, opened the eyes of the blind, cast out demons and set at liberty those who were oppressed.[3]

In Mark 13:11, Jesus told the disciples not to worry about what they would say if they were arrested for their faith: "Just say whatever is given you at the time, for it is not you speaking, but the Holy Spirit." He promised the Spirit would "illuminate the truth so that men might know the Lord. By the power of the Holy Spirit, the disciples were told they'd have the very ability to do the works of their Lord (John 14:12)."[4] If we have accepted Christ as our Savior and invited Him to dwell in our hearts, then we have everything we need to communicate Christ as we abide in Him, rely on His provision, and wait on His timing.

A natural way to communicate Christ to others is by opening the windows of our lives and letting others look in. Similar experiences and shared interests are two areas of common ground that allow us to discuss our story with others. When appropriate, recount for others your experiences, while quoting Scripture that helped you walk through a specific time they can relate to. We have all faced difficult choices, experienced great joy, or have interests we share with others.

Common Experiences

After the initial trauma, it made sense that God asked me to walk into the tragedy of my neighbor's suicide. My own mother could have taken Amelia's place twenty years prior when I battled with depression and contemplated taking my own life. That experience enabled me to assure her that it wasn't her fault and unfold the story of the gospel by telling how God rescued me from the pit of despair.

My struggle with depression has opened numerous doors for me to talk with women, teenagers, and parents of children battling with hopelessness. What are some of your life experiences that give you common ground with those in your sphere of influence?

Shared Interests

I love to scrapbook. When my husband saw how much I enjoyed it, he suggested I become a scrapbook consultant. As I prayed for God's direction with this business venture, I sensed it as a calling that would not only provide income but also a platform for ministry. In the months prior, I had been praying for a way to open my home to women in my neighborhood in hopes of building relationships. Three years later, I have a very successful business, but more important I have gained the friendship of more than twenty women who are neighbors or friends of neighbors. They gather at my house monthly to create keepsake albums. As they work with their photos, they share their stories and their hearts.

My interest in scrapbooking has opened the door for me to build relationships and communicate Christ to women I would have never met otherwise. Several have expressed interest in a neighborhood Bible study. Some have joined my business unit, and one recently indicated on a questionnaire that her greatest need right now is spiritual guidance. What is an interest of yours? Pray for creative ways to use your shared interests to communicate Christ to those in your neighborhood or workplace.

OVERCOMING FEAR IN WITNESSING

One of the greatest obstacles we face in discussing our faith is fear. At the tender age of four, my son Joshua forever changed my perspective of fear.

We had rented a house on the beach with its own pool and a large deck overlooking the ocean. Our friends John and Laura and their two children had joined us. As we returned from the beach one evening we noticed that our four-year-olds, Joshua and Steven, had disappeared. John ran back to the house. As he crossed the deck and set his eyes on the pool, he saw that Steven had fallen in. Joshua was bent over, arms outstretched, pulling Steven as hard as he could. Steven was gasping for air but continued to go under. Before John could get to the pool, he saw Joshua, who weighed eight pounds less than Steven, grab Steven's arm and yank him out of the pool. By the time I arrived, Steven was coughing up water and trembling in shock. As tears streamed down his cheeks, I noticed his face was blue and realized he had almost drowned.

That evening I tried to uncover what had happened. Joshua explained that Steven decided to rinse sand off a toy they'd been playing with and fell in the pool. I listened with pride and fear. In my mind I was asking, *What were you thinking? Why didn't you call for help? You never get in front of a drowning person; they'll drown you.* God stopped those words from coming out, and instead I calmly asked, "Joshua, what made you think you could pull Steven out?" In his most convincing tone, he said, "Mommy, I knew God would give me the strength."

Later that night I remembered Joshua's namesake verse: Joshua 1:9, "Be strong and courageous. Do not be terrified; do not be discouraged, for the Lord your God will be with you wherever you go." I imagined the Lord standing behind my son, His arms outstretched joining hands with Joshua as they pulled Steven out of the pool.

Joshua had not counted the cost. He was willing to step out in faith and trust that God would give him the strength to help a drowning friend. Many people are drowning all around us. Every time I am afraid to talk about my faith, the Lord reminds me to reach out my hands and partner with Him in what He is doing to rescue the lost.

When Peter got out of the boat and stepped onto the water, he walked in confidence, knowing Jesus was calling him and would empower him to do the impossible. God invites us to walk on water as we step out of our comfort zone and live a lifestyle of evangelism. Like Joshua we need to know that He will be with us and give us the strength. Are you willing to reach out your hand to extend the love of Christ to someone who may be drowning?

In John 1:4–5 we are told, "In him was life, and that life was the light of men. The light shines in the darkness, but the darkness has not understood it." We as Christians are called to hold out that Light. We who house the light and love of Christ can guide others to the safe harbor of God's heart. Will you step out in faith and spread the gospel by sharing with others all that He has done for you?

As you follow the ABCs of lifestyle evangelism by Abiding in Him, Building relationships with unbelievers, and Communicating Christ, my prayer is that you will experience the abundant life Jesus promised as you give your life away for the sake of others knowing Him.

Renee Swope has served in women's ministry for the past thirteen years and is Director of Heart to Heart Ministry at Forest Hill Church in Charlotte, North Carolina. She is a graduate of Florence Littauer's CLASS (Christian Leaders, Authors, and Speakers Seminar) and a certified speaker for The Proverbs 31 Ministries. Renee has written two Bible studies and has been published in "The P31 Woman" newsletter and the *Best of Proverbs 31 Ministry* book. She and her husband, J. J., have been married nine years and have two sons, Joshua and Andrew. They are the founders of It Starts In The Heart Ministry.

---

1 *Webster's New World Dictionary* (New York: Simon & Schuster, 1982).

2 John Ortberg, *If You Want to Walk on Water, You've Got to Get Out of the Boat* (Grand Rapids: Zondervan, 2001), 81.

3 Robert E. Coleman, *The Master Plan of Evangelism* (Grand Rapids: Revell, 1999), 65.

4 Ibid.

EXTENDING GOD'S LOVE GLOBALLY

Michele Rickett

I had not been out of the house since the birth of my second child. When I heard we were going to have a women's event at our church, I knew I had to go. With a two-year-old daughter and a three-month-old baby I was feeling that my world was getting a bit small. It was my own fault, I confess. I was an earth mother. I wore my children, one on the front and one on my back, while I grew organic vegetables in the backyard, baked bread, and hung clothes out to dry. With all that work, we barely left our little homestead. Don't misunderstand, I loved being home with my daughters. I was just a bit intense about the whole thing.

I had been taught that God's purposes for my life included people beyond my immediate family. I had neighbors across the street who didn't know Christ, and, of course, there was Jerusalem, Judea, and all those uttermost places to think of. I just did not know how to fit it all in. I knew enough to ask God to help me live beyond my own mailbox, at least for the sake of my daughters. I wanted them to become women who lived for God's purposes. And I had a feeling that God would start shaping them into servants by first getting their mother into shape.

My prayer was answered the night I put my children on their dad and I went to the women's event. It was a lovely evening: pretty tablecloths, flowers, a special soloist (a really good one), and then the main event. I sat really close to the platform, so I could suck the marrow out of everything God had to say to me. The speaker slowly rose to the stage after she was introduced. Ruth Finley was impressive. She had shocking white hair and blue eyes that flashed a passion for the world. This woman was captivating in her passion for the world to come to Christ. She held a globe in her quivering hands and yelled, "God, give me Czechoslovakia or I'll die!" I wanted to jump from my seat and yell too. *Where IS Czechoslovakia, anyway? And I'm not sure why it's killing us that we don't have it,* I thought. *But wherever it is, I'm with you, sister!* I began writing notes all over my program. I didn't want to forget a word of this inspiring, challenging time.

She was nowhere near finished with her audience. Ruth brought her talk right down to the personal level. *Good,* I thought. We really need to get blasted. "We do not have forever . . ." she stopped short. She looked right at me. She pointed. "No, you! You do not have forever to become the woman God wants you to be." I was horrified. Did she mean me? Excuse me? I am a very young person. I have two small babies at home. Couldn't she have looked at someone else? On my way home I argued with God, "You obviously made her point at the wrong person! I can't go off to Czechoslovakia—wherever in the world that is . . ." I was bothered. Bothered by God in a good way.

He answered my prayer by challenging me not to wait until the kids were older to focus on His agenda. I couldn't go overseas right then, but I could listen to, meet, and read about admirable women, women like Ruth Finley. From that day I began a process of seeking out women who were "on purpose" for God. In that quest, I picked up a little book that changed everything for me.

That very year, now twenty years ago, the book *Born to Lose* was written by Lorry Lutz. It was the story of a daughter of freed slaves in Alabama. Eliza George was called by God to go to Liberia and tell of Christ to those who had never heard. But she couldn't find an agency that would send a little black lady to do missions. Eliza was undaunted. She went to the women of her church and asked them to pray and sacrifice to send her. With their help Eliza got to Liberia and began teaching naked jungle children about God. She clothed them with her own blouses; she taught them without books, chairs, or a blackboard; and Eliza George was hungry most of the time. I remember hot, angry tears flowing down my face as I read about her suffering. I was so upset, I called the author.

Lorry Lutz listened to my angry questions. "How could God let a servant like Eliza suffer so?" Lorry was ready for the question. She captured a teachable moment. "Michele, I want you to consider two things. First of all, you really should finish reading the book. Secondly, perhaps your anger is just a little misplaced. Instead of being angry with God, why don't you wonder about all those women who knew about Eliza and never gave her a thought, never shared what they had with her." In that moment something was born in me. I thought, if only one woman had stood up for Eliza and reminded her sisters of her ministry, she would have had all the books, chairs, clothes, and food she needed.

After I talked with Lorry I went to my room, shut the door, and fell on my face before God. I cried out my repentance. "If ever there is a way that I can help the Eliza Georges who are suffering to serve You, just show me what to do and I'll do it." The next day I finished the book. I learned that Eliza did not know that she was feeding, clothing, and teaching the "Billy Graham" for Liberia, Agustus Marwieh. It was Gus who grew up out of the jungles and told the story to missionary Lorry Lutz.

You might think my prayer to help suffering missionaries was a bit vague. It was. I only asked God to show me what to do. You can be sure He hears the prayers of sincere hearts. He heard mine. I devoured one missions book after another. Those were the stories we told our daughters about. Those were the people we admired. And in the fullness of time, as my children began to leave home, it was time to begin the ministry that is now connecting women with resources to 2,500 of their sisters who serve in China, India, the Middle East, Southeast Asia. These are local Christian women, just like us, except they work in the hardest places of the world.

What I've learned over the last twenty years is that the global family of faith simply needs every part to do its part. Moms who are home with their children, people who work in corporations, professors who train, women who teach Bible studies. All of us who name that worthy name have something to invest in taking His love where it has not gone before . . . if only we'll focus on that worthy task.

Historically, Christian women have had a powerful impact on the mission, as chronicled in Pierce Beaver's *All Loves Excelling* and other fine books on the subject. According to recent Gordon-Conwell research, in 1900 there were forty-five women's "sending societies" of North American women working for the express purpose of sending women to lands without a gospel witness. Now, at the turn of the millennium those vehicles have vanished. Couple that fact with the tremendous growth of the numbers of Christian workers in non-Western nations, and we see that it is time for innovations for women's involvement in global outreach.

Thankfully, a new women's movement has emerged, creating relationships between women in the West with their global sisters. The goal of these women is to partner with indigenous Christian women working to make Christ known to women and children suffering all their lives without the comfort and hope of Christ. The "SIS" movement of individual women and project-oriented chapters (or societies) nationwide has focused on each one embracing a "sister" ministry among the unreached: praying for, empowering, equipping local ministry women in China, India, Africa, the Middle East, Indonesia . . . functioning as sisters in a global village. (See the appendix for information on contacting Sisters in Service.)

Women are having a powerful impact right from their homes and churches as they embrace sisters who suffer to serve, looking out for the concerns of others as more important than our own—in true Philippians 2 fashion. When Christian women awaken to collaborating, everyone benefits. I liken women in the U.S. to Queen Esther in the Bible. We have station and privileges like royalty. Our greatest privilege, like Esther's, is in leveraging all we've been given to help God's agenda, God's people. I know some modern-day Esthers. They've fully embraced projects such as small business development in India, literacy in Mali, health huts in Muslim villages, water catchments in China, pig farms, Bible training. . . . There's something for everyone, if we'll only step out, choose one place, one project, and begin to speak up for another sister . . . and so fulfill the law of Christ.

Michele Rickett has taken an active leadership role in women's ministries for more than twenty-three years. Michele directs Partners International women's ministry, Sisters In Service. In addition to an international speaking and teaching ministry, Michele has developed numerous workshops and is the author of the Bible study *Ordinary Women: Developing a Faithwalk Worth Passing On.*

PART FIVE

MAINTAINING A WOMEN'S MINISTRY

God never intended for us to journey through life alone. Women's ministry is certainly no place to do so. How exciting it is to bring other women along and help develop their leadership and ministry skills. Most women want to be a part of something that will positively mold them and help them grow and develop.

As a leader, you should be in the constant process of giving your job away. What? Giving it away? Yes, the more you develop the leadership skills of the women around you, the more your women's ministry will develop and grow. We do this through a process of "Leader/Learner" development.

Here's how it works:

Leader	*Learner*
Christlike Character ⟶	Confidence
Compassion ⟶	Connection

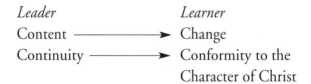

Leader   *Learner*
Content   ——————➤ Change
Continuity ——————➤ Conformity to the
                                    Character of Christ

A leader's character is where it all starts. If her *character* is Christlike, she will win the *confidence* and trust of her learner. If she is *compassionate,* then the learner will *connect* with her and trust her enough to move to the next level of listening to her content. The leader's *content* must be filled with scriptural truths and presented in a way that it equips the learner for digging deeper into Scripture for herself. Then the learner begins to *change* through the power in God's Word and her own walk with Him deepening. As this process *continues* over a period of time, the learner's character begins to *conform* to the character of Christ. She then becomes a leader and develops other learners.

It's a beautiful process, but for it to be successful we must keep our character as leaders in check. Psalm 1:1–3 says, "Blessed is the [woman] who does not walk in the counsel of the wicked or stand in the way of sinners or sit in the seat of mockers. But [her] delight is in the law of the LORD, and on his law [she] meditates day and night. [She] is like a tree planted by streams of water, which yields its fruit in season and whose leaf does not wither. Whatever [she] does prospers."

I pray that as we walk through this last section, you feel equipped from all you've read thus far and will now be inspired to maintain the incredible ministry God is entrusting to you.

TWENTY-ONE

DEVELOPING LEADERS WITHIN YOUR MINISTRY

Susan Miller

I was overwhelmed as I entered the room filled with godly women I had admired and respected for years. These were women who were leaders in ministry, teachers of God's Word, and eloquent speakers. They knew the Bible well, could quote Scripture from memory, and could speak without notes. Their lives were etched with a knowledge of Christ and the strength that comes from a daily walk with Him.

As a new leader my first thought was, *What am I doing here? I feel so inadequate!* My second thought was, *Me? A leader . . . they have asked the wrong person; I don't belong here!* At that moment, my heart began to pound with a sense of panic, and I felt the urge to disappear into the woodwork.

Perhaps you've been in that same room and felt those same

feelings as I did many years ago. I've come a long way in my journey of leadership since that day. I've learned a lot along the way from others who have gone before me as inspiring leaders. But most of all, I've learned from the master of leadership, the most inspiring leader I could ever follow—Jesus Christ. He is the One who set the example and then took me by the hand to show me the way. It is from an intimate relationship with Him that I have been inspired and equipped to do that which I could not do in my own strength. It is the personal touch of my Master's hand with which I attempt to lead others.

Perhaps you are a new or potential leader, looking for reassurance that you can do this thing called "leadership." Perhaps you just need a little renewal as a leader who feels on overload. Come and sit by my side in the next few pages. I will encourage you in your journey to become a leader. I will tell you some things I've learned about developing leaders in ministry. Remember, we aren't alone on the path to leadership. Christ not only shows us the way through His example, He paves the way with His Word!

OUR PATTERN FOR LEADERSHIP

First things first. What a relief for me when I realized I didn't have to figure out how to be a leader all by myself! "Come, follow me," Christ tells us (Matthew 19:21). Those three simple words changed my attitude, my heart, and my direction as a leader. The "first thing" I needed to do was to follow the example of Jesus. "Do not be called leaders; for One is your Leader, that is, Christ. But the greatest among you shall be your servant" (Matthew 23:10–11 NASB). Jesus redefined the privilege of leadership for me when I understood that to lead is to serve. By His example and His Word, I began to see that I am to lead others through a servant's heart and with a serving spirit.

I don't consider myself a great leader. I'm just an ordinary woman who is in a privileged position to serve others through my leadership.

I want to represent my Lord the very best that I can. There are days I feel I've served well and there are days I beg for a second chance. Let me share with you some leadership principles I've learned over the years through observing the life of Jesus Christ. They will be invaluable to you as you are training and developing leaders.

Choose the women you want to develop. In Mark 3:13 (NASB) we are told that "He . . . summoned those whom He Himself wanted." Pray for God's guidance about whom you might choose.

Show them what to do and how to do it. Jesus was so good at teaching through demonstration. From praying to washing feet, I think He was a master at "show and tell"!

Share your life with them. Mark 3:14 tells us that "he appointed twelve . . . that they might be with him." Let them see the real you. Be vulnerable in sharing your life, and you will become more credible.

Involve them in ministry. Jesus involved His disciples in so much that He did, from passing out bread to baptizing. Women love to feel a part of what's going on, and involvement gives them ownership in that ministry.

Delegate authority. When you assign a task, by all means don't forget to give the authority to do it. Jesus trusted His disciples with a task and blessed them with authority.

Develop a team. When Jesus sent out His disciples, they knew they were not alone. He sent them out two by two (Mark 6:7). When you have two or more women together, they can complement each other and excel in their own area of giftedness.

Encourage accountability. Mark 6:30 tells us "the apostles gathered around Jesus and reported to him all they had done and taught." Meet with your leaders for feedback. Stay in communication and in touch. You need to know how to best teach, lead, and minister to your women through their accountability to you.

If I want to develop leaders within ministry, I must keep my own heart Christ-centered and my motives on track with His purpose. As a servant-leader, some of my checkpoints are:

Am I leading from my heart? I want to lead out of joy, enthusiasm, and passion, not duty!

Am I available, approachable, and accessible as a leader? Jesus certainly was! He demonstrated throughout Scripture the importance of a personal and relational touch in ministry. I try to always carry my "AAA" card with me.

Am I too busy with my own agenda, or am I listening to God? It's easy for me to come to God with my own ministry plans. I need to remind myself daily to seek God's direction, lay my ministry at His feet, and then, be still and listen.

Am I committed to Christ? Being a leader is not about me; it is about God. It is not about my ego; it is about giving Him the honor and glory.

Am I growing in Christ through His Word? In leadership, I can only take women as far as I've been. If I don't deepen my walk with the Lord and get to know Him more intimately, then I'm just "talking the talk."

I am constantly reminded that the women around me are reading the pages of my life. Am I the kind of leader they would want to follow? So much of developing potential leaders will be through my example, my words, my actions, the way that I relate to and treat others. It all begins with my desire to imitate the principles and truths of the Master of leadership . . . Jesus Christ.

QUALITIES TO LOOK FOR IN A LEADER

When I'm in a group of women, I will often find myself quietly looking around for someone with leadership potential. I've come up with some identifiable qualities that might be helpful to you too. Don't misunderstand me, I don't check a list but rather watch those who might exemplify these traits.

Are they faithful, available, and teachable?
Are they dependent on God and in His Word?

Are they committed?
Are they visionary?
Are they goal oriented?
Are they positive and enthusiastic?
Are they transparent?
Do they bring God's truth to life?

Remember: Godliness over giftedness, and faithfulness is more important than excellence!

THE PERSONAL TOUCH IN LEADERSHIP

The value of balancing leadership skills with a personal touch and a relational connection is immeasurable. In 1995 I founded a ministry for women who are going through the transition and adjustment of moving. N.E.W. Ministries is now touching the lives of women internationally, giving them hope and encouragement after a major move. Our ministry office is staffed by some twenty-five volunteers, all of them women who have gone through the experience of moving and relocating. I also have the privilege of leading the NEWcomers Ministry at my home church along with a leadership team of four women.

All of these women are more than volunteers to me; they are leaders in their area of responsibility and in their area of giftedness. I know their life stories and their families. They have been guests in my home, and they live in my heart. I celebrate their joys and cry with them in their pain. We have prayed together and rejoiced together. They have seen me at my best and at my worst, when things are going smooth and when they are stressful. And yet, regardless of any God-given leadership skills I might have, I know that this ministry would not be where it is today without my taking the time to build relationships and give the personal touch of encouragement, affirmation, care, and value to these precious women who lead and serve in this ministry.

213

Consider some of these practical ways you might add a personal touch and build a relational connection with your potential leaders:

Give them "TLC." May your "Tender Loving Care" become "Transforming the Love of Christ." Demonstrate God's love through your words and actions.

Listen with your heart. Women have a need to be heard. You impart value by listening.

Know their needs. For example, some women have a need for recognition, whereas some may have a need for affirmation in what they are doing.

Recognize their accomplishments. Verbally applaud them privately and in public.

Show appreciation. A gift, a card, even a phone call to say thank you shows your gratefulness.

Give support. Convey your support through words, a note, or an action. It is both comforting and encouraging to know someone has come alongside in a situation.

Be nonjudgmental. Sometimes extra grace is required!

Offer learning opportunities. Conferences, seminars, workshops, tapes, and books are great tools for growth. We are never too old to keep learning.

Develop their potential. Help women grow and develop to their full potential. Tell them you believe in them and their abilities. Identify goals and areas of giftedness. Make someone look good at what she does.

Be an encourager. This is where I bring out my pom-poms! Be someone's cheerleader. We all need someone to cheer us on to victory.

Be flexible. People appreciate some flexibility when something unplanned or unscheduled happens.

Be sensitive. I can get busy working my list and forget that someone around me might be going through a crisis and need prayer, a listening heart, a few moments of my time, or a hug. It goes without saying what is more important.

Know how to motivate individually. What motivates one leader may not motivate another. Understand each person and her own style of learning.

Convey warmth and caring. Genuinely communicate your care and interest. Let your words and actions be in harmony.

Participate in their lives. Remember special occasions, remember their family's names, celebrate together, cry together, pray for them, follow up on important family events, and follow through on your commitments and plans made together.

I look around me every day and see how God has done incredible things in the lives of so many of the newcomers He has transplanted into our church. Many are women who thought they could never do the things they have done or could never become the women they are today. Women who have bloomed as leaders, teachers, event planners, ministry coordinators, ministry assistants, speakers . . . and the list goes on. What a privilege to stand in the wings and cheer them on to be all they can be for Jesus Christ as they serve Him in leadership!

Won't you join me now in this wonderful opportunity as we invest in the lives of women who will be our leaders for tomorrow?

Susan Miller is the President and Founder of N.E.W. Ministries, Inc., a ministry for women going through the adjustment and transition of moving. She is the author of *After the Boxes Are Unpacked . . . Moving On After Moving In* and *The New Neighbor Pocket Guide.* She was also a featured author of the *Renewing the Heart* book and calendar. Susan has appeared as a guest on many radio programs and speaks to churches and women's groups internationally.

TWENTY-TWO

THE POWER OF
ENCOURAGEMENT

Sharon Jaynes

I was flipping through my local newspaper and noticed a calendar of events for the week. For the first time, I perused the list to see what was happening in my fair city. Then a stark reality hit me and I began to count. In that one week, 146 support group meetings were scheduled—everything from Alcoholics Anonymous to Codependents Anonymous to Recovery from Food Addiction. Then over to the side a note said, "If you're looking for a support group not listed here, call . . ." Once again I was struck with how desperately people need the gift of encouragement and how they will go just about anywhere to get it.

Women need encouragement as never before. Because of the trends in our society, they no longer have the family support and sense of community support that was prevalent just a few generations ago. We once sang, "Over the river and through the woods, to Grandmother's house we go." But because we live in such a transient society, Grandmother's house in many cases is no longer over the river and through the woods, but across several state lines. And when you get to Grandma's house, she's probably not at home but out with her roller blading club, on an Alaskan cruise, or at water aerobics class. Grandmothers today live very busy and active lives of their own.

Not only do women not have the support of family readily available as in times past, they many times do not have the support of neighbors and a sense of community where they live. Where we once had a welcome mat, we now have a warning sticker telling those who approach our doors that we have an alarm system. Many of us don't even know our neighbors right next door.

Never before in the history of the world do people have such ready access to others. We have e-mail, instant messaging, call waiting, call forwarding, caller ID, and call return. We clip on beepers, tote cell phones, and even wear headphones so as to not miss a call while driving or working. And yet, women feel more isolated and alone than ever before.

A Kansas City newspaper ad said: "I will listen to you, uninterrupted, for 30 minutes, for $5."[1] The person placing the ad said he was inundated with calls. Another article in a local newspaper wrote of a "Friend for Hire." For $500 a month, you could hire a personal development coach. Basically, these life coaches admitted they mostly listened and occasionally gave advice.[2] I think this inborn need to know others and be known is the pull of shows like Oprah's. Many people spend five hours a week with Oprah, when they may not spend five minutes getting to know the person right next door. The person next door may be more interesting, but getting to know her is a lot of work, and TV is easy.

These are just a few of the reasons women need encouragement today and some of the ways they are seeking to have that need met. As Christians, we can offer so much more.

THE ENCOURAGEMENT OF WOMEN

What exactly is encouragement? Webster defines it: to give courage or confidence, to raise the hopes of, to help on by sympathetic advice and interest, to promote or stimulate. William Barclay explains our need to encourage this way:

> One of the highest of human duties is the duty of encouragement. It is easy to laugh at men's ideas; it is easy to pour cold water on their enthusiasm; it is easy to discourage others. The world is full of discouragers. We have a Christian duty to encourage one another. Many a time a word of praise or thanks or appreciation or cheer has kept a man on his feet. Blessed is the man [or woman] who speaks such a word.[3]

All through Scripture, we see how God placed women together in relationship to encourage one another. Just as God sent Mary to Elizabeth and Ruth to Naomi, He continues to place women together for mutual support, accountability, and friendship. As you begin to build your women's ministry, the women on the leadership team who feel encouraged themselves will be the ones who stay for the longest periods of time. If their emotional "buckets" are empty, they will have a difficult time filling others.

I love the story in 1 Kings 17 in which God sent the prophet Elijah to be ministered to by a widow. Elijah had been living by a river, which had dried up, so God led him to a widow to feed and house him. When Elijah approached her and asked for food, she explained that she was just now picking up sticks to start a fire. She had only enough flour in her bowl and enough oil in her jar for one more cake of bread. She was about to prepare this last supper for her and her son, and then they were going to lie down and die. Elijah assured her if she would fix him a little cake first, then one for herself and her son, her bowl would not go empty and her jar would not run dry until the drought was over.

The widow followed Elijah's requests, and her bowl and jar did not run dry, but God miraculously supplied her needs. What a beautiful picture of Jesus' words in Luke 6:38: "Give, and it will be given to you. A good measure, pressed down, shaken together and running over, will be poured into your lap. For with the measure you use, it will be measured to you."

I like to picture giving the gift of encouragement being like dipping out of a bucket. We each have a bucket of encouragement. Some people have little in their buckets, and some have abundance. The trick is, when you dip out of your bucket to encourage someone, the Lord pours back into your bucket. However, there are many who are running low and they try to fill their buckets by dipping out of others' buckets— hurting others to elevate themselves. Unfortunately, that person will always have an empty bucket as it leaks out or evaporates immediately. The only way to fill our encouragement bucket is to share it with others and watch the Lord fill us to overflowing.

PAUL'S ENCOURAGEMENT

Perhaps one of the greatest encouragers in the Bible was Paul, writer of more than half the New Testament. In each of his letters to the various churches, Paul began with encouraging words. "[I] do not cease giving thanks for you" (Ephesians 1:16 NASB). "I thank my God in all my remembrance of you, always offering prayer with joy in my every prayer for you all" (Philippians 1:3–4 NASB). "I have you in my heart" (Philippians 1:7 NASB). "We always thank God, the Father of our Lord Jesus Christ, when we pray for you" (Colossians 1:3).

Even though Paul's letters began with encouraging words, their primary purpose was to exhort, instruct, and, yes, correct. He was never known as a pushover, but his reproofs were always wrapped in love.

Paul was a wonderful encourager to his son in the Lord, Timothy, telling Timothy that he believed in him. Paul gave Timothy great responsibility and reassured the youth of his confidence that he could do the job.

Timothy was a young man when Paul sent him to resolve several serious problems in the church at Ephesus. No doubt Paul's words of encouragement built confidence in the lad. "Don't let anyone look down on you because you are young, but set an example for the believers in speech, in life, in love, in faith and in purity" (1 Timothy 4:12). Paul sent young Timothy and assured him that he trusted him and that he knew he could handle the job. All the while, Paul was on the sidelines cheering, "GO TIMOTHY! You can do it!" And Timothy did.

In Hebrews 12:1 the writer encourages us, "Let us run with perseverance the race marked out for us." We as Christians are running the great race of life. As a mother, I have watched the power of encouragement at sporting events of every sort. I've watched runners quicken their pace when they heard a word of cheer. I have seen a fallen youngster rise up and continue toward the goal when coaxed by the crowd. I've witnessed runners slacken when opposing teams' fans hurled insults.

ENCOURAGEMENT TO ENDURE

When my son became a cross-country runner, I learned more about the power of encouragement in this sport of endurance. As a runner nears the end of a footrace, his throat burns, his legs ache, and his whole body cries out for him to stop. That's when the cheers of the friends and fans are the most important. Their encouragement helps him push through the pain to the finish. In the same way, a word of encouragement, offered at just the right moment, may help someone run the race of life with endurance. A word of praise may make the difference between someone's finishing well or collapsing along the way. As a ministry leader, your words may mean the difference between a sister's running well or collapsing along the way.

Businessman Charles Schwab said, "I have yet to find the man—however exalted his station—who did not do better work and put forth greater effort under a spirit of approval than under a spirit of criticism."[4] This concept is not only true in the business world but in our homes, in our communities, and in our ministries.

Here are a few ways to encourage the women on your leadership teams.

* Ask good questions. Avoid the empty, "How are you?" and replace it with, "How can I pray for you today?"

* Pray with them, not just for them.

* Listen without giving advice.

* Let them repeat details if they are going through a crisis.

* Write encouraging notes often.

* Observe their interests. Then when you see something that fits that person, buy it as a gift. It shows that you have been listening. For example, if Debbie loves bunnies, purchase gifts with a bunny theme.

* Remember friends at tender times. For example, if a friend has a miscarriage, note the date on your calendar and send her a card on the one-year anniversary of her loss.

✤ Keep a basket of post cards by your Bible and send notes to people when you pray for them simply saying, "I prayed for you today."

✤ Praise members of your team publicly for a job well done.

✤ Give someone responsibility and then allow her the freedom to do it her way.

✤ Send your team leaders on "continuing education field trips." Invest in their spiritual and emotional growth. For example: send them to leadership classes, spiritual gifts courses, or public speaking seminars.

✤ Have a fun day when the team does a nonministry-related activity, and simply enjoys one another's company. Have someone underwrite the expenses so it will be a true treat for all involved.

These are just a few ideas to get you started. I suggest that you write Luke 6:31 at the top of a page: "Do to others as you would have them do to you." Then make your own list. Write down some things that you secretly have desired for someone to do to encourage you, and then begin doing those things to encourage others!

Women love beautiful, valuable jewels. Rubies, diamonds, and emeralds are precious and hard to find. But I propose that a true encourager is much more valuable, sought after, and beautiful than these. You desire to be a treasure? Invest in someone's life. You desire to be remembered? Do something memorable to build up another person. You desire to have fulfilled dreams? Help others fulfill their aspirations. You desire to have a blazing passion for Christ in your life? Fan the smoldering embers of someone's spiritual life and watch the flames ignite.

Is encouragement easy? Not on your life. Chuck Swindoll said it well:

It takes courage, tough minded courage, to trust God, to believe in ourselves, and to reach a hand to others. But what a beautiful way to live. I know of no one more needed, more valuable, more Christ-like than the person who is committed to encouragement. In spite of others' actions. Regardless of others' attitudes. It is the musical watchword that takes the grind out of living—encouragement.[5]

Sharon Jaynes is Vice President of Proverbs 31 Ministries, Inc., and co-host for the ministry's international radio segments. She is a feature writer for the Proverbs 31 monthly newsletter, author of many books, including *Being a Great Mom, Raising Great Kids; Seven Life Principles for Every Woman;* and *Celebrating a Christ-Centered Christmas,* and an inspirational speaker for women's events from coast to coast.

[1] Dennis Rainey, *Staying Close* (Dallas: Word, 1989), 216.

[2] Mark Price, "Get a Life," *The Charlotte Observer,* 1 November 1998.

[3] William Barclay, *The Letter to the Hebrews, The Daily Study Bible* (Edinburgh: St. Andrews Press, 1955), 137–38.

[4] Zig Ziglar, *Raising Positive Kids in a Negative World* (New York: Ballantine, 1989), 54.

[5] Charles R. Swindoll, *Encourage Me* (Grand Rapids: Zondervan, 1982), 90.

TWENTY-THREE

PRACTICAL WAYS TO DEAL WITH TEAM CONFLICT

Sheryl DeWitt

Carla was an attractive, vivacious, intelligent, creative thirty-two-year-old woman who came across as being very confident. She had recently joined our ministry and had been a real asset to our team. I was surprised when she burst into my office with tears streaming down her face. "I thought this was a Christian ministry. I didn't think I would have to face the same hurts here that I did in my secular job." The tears were flowing as she tried to speak to me. When she calmed down, she proceeded to tell me, "I expected the secular world to gossip about me behind my back. But when my Christian sisters who proclaim to love me spread gossip, it hurts me deeply."

Three of the eight women whom Carla worked with were talking about her. They were gossiping among themselves about the way she dressed and stating that they thought she always had to be the center of attention. These cruel words had gotten back to Carla and crushed her.

When I talked to these three women, it was obvious that they were jealous of Carla's appearance and personality. Because she had such an outgoing and warm personality, she did draw others to her. These women were competing for attention and losing the race toward popularity. They were comparing themselves and found themselves lacking. Insecurity was fueling the anger that they were taking out on Carla by criticizing her to one another.

Working with women for many years, I have seen that three of the biggest conflicts that woman seem to struggle with are jealousy, gossip, and competition. We all want to be affirmed for who we are and what we have done. If we feel that someone else is getting more praise than we are, it is very easy to find ourselves being resentful and seeking to tear down the person who is getting the praise we want.

How this grieves the Lord. My two sons are only twenty months apart. They are either best friends or worst enemies, depending on the moment. Nothing makes me grieve more as a mom than when they are fighting and tearing each other down. My younger son, Jonathan, is a straight A student and has one or two close friends, but is a little on the shy side. My older son is the friendliest young man I have ever seen. He never meets a stranger, and our phone is constantly ringing with calls for him, but academically he struggles. When they have gotten angry with each other, Jonathan will call Christopher "stupid," and Christopher will tell Jonathan that he is not popular at school. They both attack each other's weakness because they are jealous of the other's strength. This breaks my heart because I see two precious little boys whom I truly love and who are gifted in different areas. This is what was happening with Carla. The other women were attacking her strengths because of their own insecurity. This breaks the Lord's heart when He sees His precious daughters belittling and hurting each other because they are ungrateful for the gifts God gave them and want what God gave someone else.

The other day Christopher was struggling with homework and being very hard on himself. I noticed Jonathan went over to his older brother and showed him a shortcut to the math problem he was having difficulty with. When it was bedtime, Christopher came out to me and showed me a letter that Jonathan had left on his pillow. It said, "Chris, I think you are the smartest brother and I am proud of the way that you always make people feel good about themselves because you are so kind. I am very thankful you are my big brother. I look up to you. Love, Jon." This note deeply touched my thirteen-year-old son. It had me in tears. I was so pleased to see my children encouraging each other and working together, each recognizing and encouraging the other person's strengths.

This is God's desire for women. He wants us to see value in the different gifts He has given us and to encourage each other in these gifts. How it touches His heart when we remember we are working together for His glory and not our own.

THE INEVITABILITY OF CONFLICT

Whenever two or more people are asked to work together, conflict will occur. Bringing together different backgrounds, ideas, and expectations virtually guarantees that conflict will arise. Conflict is not a bad thing. It is the way we deal with conflict that can make it a strengthening time or a painful time for us.

Carla's initial response to the conflict she was having with the other women was to be hurt. Then the anger came. She was ready to leave our ministry and go somewhere else. Her expectation that Christians should react to her in a more loving way led to great disappointment.

Withdrawing from a conflict is not always the best solution. When we pretend that things are OK or ignore them, bitterness and resentment build up. If we have a cancer and choose to ignore it, it will not go away. Instead it will grow and, if not treated, could potentially be deadly. This is the same way with conflict. Once a conflict arises it must be dealt with or it will ultimately harm the person who is internalizing, destroy the relationship, and alienate other Christians.

After teaching conflict resolution in my private practice for corporations, marriages, and in other relationships, I have learned that the best way to deal with conflict is to try to prevent it. Second, when conflicts that are unavoidable happen, it is critical to know how to handle them swiftly.

THE PREVENTION OF CONFLICT

Prevention takes place by learning to encourage and build up those you work with. Women have a need to be affirmed and nurtured for who they are. Most women who end up on the couch in my counseling office feel unappreciated and unloved. They struggle with self-worth and feeling that they are not valuable. When a woman has an inaccurate view of herself, this is when comparison takes place. The thing that has always amazed me is that when we compare ourselves to someone else, we usually compare our weaknesses to his or her strengths. Rarely do we compare strength for strength. Therefore, comparison is deadly to our self-image because we always end up on the losing side. This leads to jealousy of others and many times encourages us to gossip. Somehow venting our dislike of another person seems to build us up for the moment. This is a deceitful way of thinking, because realistically we do not feel better. Instead, we hurt others. When you are able to help women recognize their worth in Christ and appreciate and affirm the job they do for the ministry, they will be less likely to compete for attention and should not feel the need to compare themselves to the other women they work with.

AFFIRMATION AND GRATITUDE

One of the ways we did this in our ministry was to teach the women how to verbally affirm one another. We all memorized Ephesians 4:29, "Do not let any unwholesome talk come out of your mouths, but only what is helpful for building others up according to their needs, that it may benefit those who listen." I remember hearing Florence Littauer speaking on this verse. She talks of our words as silver boxes. Every word we speak to another person should be a gift to him. It should be like giving him a silver box. She goes on to give an example of what she means. Her son came home from school excited. "Mom, my teacher said you must be very proud because I was such a sweet little boy!"

She recalls responding to him, "Well, she doesn't see you at home, does she?" She remembers regretting the words as soon as they came out of her mouth. The teacher had given her son a silver box, and she had taken it away.

When a woman weighs her words to see if they will be silver boxes to the hearer, it is amazing how gossip halts. We were proactive in teaching the woman to say things to each other such as, "Carla, I really appreciate your enthusiasm and caring heart." Or, "Joan, you are so helpful. Thank you for always being aware when the copy machine needs paper. I really appreciate your thoughtfulness." Another way appreciation was expressed was by leaving little notes in each other's boxes. It is amazing the power an encouraging word can have.

Another thing we worked on together, as a team, was how to be thankful for what gifts God gave us and not compare ourselves with others. We memorized Philippians 4:8, "Finally, brothers, whatever is true, whatever is noble, whatever is right, whatever is pure, whatever is lovely, whatever is admirable—if anything is excellent or praiseworthy —think about such things." As we begin to think of the blessings that God has given us and thank Him for them, the comparison and jealousy go out the door. We also learned to focus on the good qualities that

God gave each team member, instead of dwelling on the weaknesses. It was wonderful how this activity boosted teamwork and brought the women closer as each of them validated and encouraged her fellow team workers.

RESOLVING CONFLICT

Along with edifying, encouraging, and affirming each other, we still had to learn how to deal with the inevitable conflicts that came along. One of the most important rules of dealing with conflict is to deal with it as soon as possible. Clint and Lisa had been married for ten months. Because Clint was his own boss, they were able to meet every Thursday for lunch. It started out as a wonderful time being together. But Lisa had a habit of being late. At first it didn't bother Clint too much. But after weeks of having to wait for his dear wife twenty-five to thirty minutes, he began to be resentful. His time was valuable and he had scheduled appointments after his lunch date. Her tardiness made him rush to the next appointment. However, he did not tell Lisa this. After a couple months of this, he began canceling lunch dates with her. She was hurt and confused. Finally in anger she confronted him on not making her a priority. At once the months of irritation exploded out of his mouth. The words he said were very hurtful and caught her completely off guard. He apologized quickly, but the damage had already been done. It took them quite a while to get over their hard feeling for each other. It would have been much more beneficial to their relationship if he had been honest with her at first. It also would have had less time to build up all the venom and anger that he spewed out to her.

So some helpful tips in resolving conflict are:

1. Deal with conflicts as soon as possible to avoid magnifying grudges.

2. Affirm the other women in your group publicly and, when it is necessary to confront, do it privately and confidentially.

3. Discuss your grievance with the person who has offended you and not with others in your office.

4. Confront the issues and never attack the person.

5. Be clear in expressing your true feelings. "That hurt my feelings"; "I was embarrassed when you said that to me."

6. Listen carefully to what the other person is saying, and try to understand her point of view.

7. Be quick to forgive if you have been hurt, or quick to ask forgiveness if you have hurt someone else.

8. Remember, you do not have to *like* everyone you work with or become his or her best friend. But you are commanded to love others. Treat them with the same kindness and concern you would want from them.

9. If necessary, come up with a plan of action that will prevent the situation from happening again. That may be setting boundaries, redefining roles, etc.

10. Remember that we are called to be peacemakers. It is our job to edify and build up our sisters and trust God for the results. Confrontation is for healing the relationship, not winning. Dr. Paul Meier and Dr. Frank Minirth stated, "In any conflict, the only real winners are the ones who learn how to manage that conflict and bring about a positive, constructive resolution. When we approach conflict with courage, honesty, and love for the other person, conflict is no longer the enemy of relationships. It becomes our ally."

Instead of running away as Carla originally wanted to do, she met individually with each of the women who had hurt her. She told them how hurt she was and listened to them express their sorrow for hurting her. Two asked her forgiveness and discussed how to build a better relationship with her in the future. The third woman has a difficult time relating to Carla, and they decided that even though they would never be best friends they would treat each other with kindness and deal with rubs immediately. Each of the women is committed to verbally and in small tangible ways build each other up. It has not been perfect, but the small irritations have been replaced with women who truly care for each other and are working for a common goal . . . to truly *love* the people they have been called to minister to.

Sheryl DeWitt is the Professor for Family Life Studies at Focus on the Family Institute as well as a counselor for Focus on the Family. She has been in private practice for more than seventeen years working with individuals, couples, and families. As a counselor, she has taught and supervised interns and other counselors. She has been a popular speaker at parenting conferences and has conducted business mediation with different companies.

TWENTY-FOUR

NETWORKING WITH OTHER WOMEN'S MINISTRY LEADERS

Pat Davis

Linda served on the staff of a metropolitan church as the Director of Women's Ministries. She was a talented, dynamic woman who loved God, had a passion to minister to women, and was leading a growing ministry; but there were times when she felt isolated and frustrated with some of the challenges of ministry. She wished that she could talk with some other directors of women's ministries, women who could relate, listen in confidence, understand, offer encouragement, exchange ideas, and pray together. She needed a safe place where she could be vulnerable and real.

As a ministry leader have you ever experienced similar feelings? Maybe you have felt that you just need someone to talk with, someone in the trenches like you. Someone to bounce ideas off, someone who would understand, and someone to pat you on the shoulder and say, "You can do it!" or, "Good job." If you answered yes, then I want to tell you "the rest of the story."

One day in the fall of 1990, Linda decided to take action. She picked up the telephone and called several churches and invited the directors/chairpersons of women's ministries to come to a Friday morning meeting in her office. A small group gathered on the appointed day, and as they talked, the women discovered they had some of the same needs. They brainstormed together on how to fill this void and came up with the idea for the Leaders Group that would meet the needs identified by the women. This was the birth of what eventually became known as LIFT: Leaders In Fellowship Together, a community-wide networking organization for leaders in women's ministries.

LIFT has made quite a journey over the past decade—with enough unexpected curves in the road and potholes in the pavement to keep us focused. But those of us on the journey have loved the ride as we have grown to minister to more than two hundred ministry leaders.

Perhaps your community needs a LIFT. If so, come aboard as I retrace our route—chuckholes and all.

TAKING FIRST STEPS

Under Linda Christ's direction, the Leaders Group developed a plan of action with the stated purpose "To provide an opportunity for leaders of women's ministries to come together for spiritual and personal encouragement and prayer. To create a forum for sharing ideas, challenges, and solutions common to their ministries." The Leaders Group met five times a year for two hours on Friday mornings. Since the group numbered five to six in attendance, each attendee would have the freedom to talk about the joys and challenges of her ministry, ask for resource assistance, seek advice for handling difficult situations, or even weep (yes, sometimes that happened) for fifteen minutes. At the end of the time the attendees would pray for each other and the needs expressed. I became a member of this group in 1991 just before assuming the volunteer position as Director of Women's Ministries at a large church in the area.

Were there benefits to being a part of this group? Yes, and they were many!

❧ We found a safe place to be vulnerable, a place to be heard by nonjudgmental peers who listened without any hidden agendas.

❧ We had a place for mutual encouragement and prayer support, as well as new ministry ideas and suggestions for "how-to's."

❧ One of the unexpected by-products of our gatherings was the deep friendships we developed.

A significant change occurred in 1992 when Linda resigned her position as Director of Women's Ministries at her church, stepped down from her role as leader, and passed the baton to me. Why me? I had experienced the benefits and value of a networking organization. While living in Southern California I was a member of NEWIM (Network of Evangelical Women in Ministry), a nonprofit organization with a mission to strengthen women who minister to women. That experience created a great desire in me to develop a similar organization in the Phoenix area using some of the ideas of NEWIM but adapting them to the culture of Phoenix. I invited the Leaders Group to meet in my home instead of in a church setting. A group of leaders from six churches began meeting in my home. Soon other ministry leaders learned by word of mouth about the Leaders Group, and the group increased in size, creating a need for change and flexibility.

The following year, with our numbers passing fifteen, it was evident we needed to "take the next step." I invited three women of the Leaders Group to form a leadership team with me. We four were each gifted differently: in organization, in personal caring, in teaching, and in vision. We respected each other, worked well together, and shared the same heart and vision for the Leaders Group. We were committed to the development of the Leaders Group and knew God had called us to this task, even though each of us was actively serving in our respective churches. Two of us were volunteer directors of women's ministries in our churches Two were women's ministry committee members in their respective women's ministry programs.

DEVELOPING OUR VISION

Just what would be involved in this next step? How would we accommodate growth? How would we reach out to other leaders in our community? The leadership team met to strategize about our future, clarifying just who we were, what would we do, and why and how we would do it.

We faced a variety of questions, which included,

* Would growth be limited to directors/chairpersons of women's ministries, or would we be more inclusive and invite women's ministry committee members? We knew that the deep intimacy of the original group was going to be somewhat sacrificed at the expense of broadening the audience of those women who could benefit from the group. Would it be worth the trade-off?

* Was there a way to preserve some level of intimacy, and how could we do that?

* How would our format change, and what would it look like?

* The question of money—we had none! What would be our financial plan?

Keeping in mind the purpose of the Leaders Group, the leadership team answered five questions:

Who Are We?

We chose to be an inclusive group—inviting all leaders in women's ministries. In our area, in 1993, only a handful of churches employed a director of women's ministries as a paid staff position. Most churches had a volunteer women's ministry committee with the position of chairperson rotating each year. We wanted all these leaders to have a place where ministry teams could attend together and "catch the vision" for ministry at the same time, a place to be real and to learn together.

What Would We Do, Why, and How Would We Do It?

In determining just what we would do at our meetings, we began with our purpose statement: "encouragement for your heart and soul." In giving the meetings more structure we knew that we would have to manage the tension and maintain the balance, between time at each meeting for women to connect and build friendships and time for teaching, training, and equipping. We decided that a networking time and a prayer time would be a part of each meeting, as well as a seminar-style teaching time.

What about losing the intimacy that the early Leaders Group shared? With time for women to connect and network being built into each meeting, the Leaders Group became a platform for ministry peers to develop a small group. Intimacy could still take place—but outside the Leaders Group meeting. For example: Two ministry leaders in two neighboring churches set time aside each week to meet for discussion and prayer; two ministry leaders touch base each week by phone; leaders go to lunch together following a group meeting. The Leaders Group meeting helped "set the stage" for more intimate relationships, and the women made it happen.

Benefits: We keyed into our organizational values: prayer, building friendships, networking, and encouraging leaders.

We became committed to the balance of encouragement and equipping in our planning.

We continued to value ministering to the "whole woman" and selected topics each year that would reflect our values of spiritual growth, personal growth, leadership growth, and ministry how-to's. Announcements at each meeting informed attendees of future meetings, women's ministry conferences offered in Arizona or on the West Coast, and events sponsored by local church women's ministries open to attendees. We would also include a display table at each meeting with current books relating to women, growth, and women's ministries. We had a place for churches to display samples of brochures, ministry ideas to help and encourage others, and an updated list of attendees for networking purposes. We included speaker referral forms completed by group attendees that gave names of speakers that they would recommend, topics, how to contact them, and costs.

The benefits of these changes provided a place for women to connect and to be encouraged as well as to receive practical ministry helps and leadership training.

Where Would We Do It?

To encourage leaders who were attending the meetings to take some ownership in the Leaders Group, we asked the directors of women's ministries at various churches represented in the group to volunteer to host one of the five meetings a year. Hosting a meeting meant preparing for a mini-event, providing such things as nametags, table decorations, light refreshments. The leadership team of the Leaders Group would plan and lead the meeting. The women's ministries director who served as our hostess for the meeting would be invited to talk about the women's ministries program at her church.

This provided a time for discussing new ideas and learning what was happening in other women's ministries in the area. It made women feel included and provided mutual support. We also used this platform to invite leaders attending our meeting to attend the women's ministries events of sister churches.

How Would We Finance It?

We knew that we needed to develop a financial plan for the Leaders Group, but the truth was that we did not have much in the way of finances. A short-term decision was made to trust God for the finances that came from the offerings collected at each meeting in addition to occasional donations.

We did not have a formal membership fee. We wanted to develop a strong base of women and churches that regularly attended the Leaders Group, and to earn a reputation in the community for excellence and reliability, before growing financially. We made a conscious and philosophical decision to put people before money. We understood that lack of a nonprofit status was a barrier to significant contributions. Our long-range goal was to someday have nonprofit status.

Our short-term plan for covering our costs included collecting an offering at each meeting and working to keep costs at a minimum. The leadership team worked out of their homes using their own computers to send mailings to attendees. In the beginning we gave small gifts as a "thank you" to invited speakers. As our numbers increased, we began giving small monetary gifts.

How Would We Grow?

We made a deliberate decision to continue to grow by "word of mouth." We wanted to grow slowly, growing a broad base of women, and to grow deep, developing commitments to one another.

The benefit to attendees was an opportunity for friendship to develop and grow. The benefit to the Leaders Group was commitment on the part of the attendees.

During this time our volunteer leadership team met on a regular basis for praying, strategizing, and more praying. In order to minister to the whole woman, we would plan topics and speakers that would speak to the personal and spiritual development of leaders as well as to ministry how-to's.

I can almost hear you asking—where did you find your speakers? The leadership team attended four different churches in the area, and we each drew from our own networks. Speakers graciously contributed their time to our meetings and to our organization because of friendships with our leaders and support of our mission. Networking with women's ministry leaders from many local churches was an added benefit to our speakers. We invited women (and our favorite man, Dr. Norm Wakefield of Phoenix Seminary) because of their love of God, passion for ministry, expertise and knowledge, and skill in communicating that knowledge. Over the years, some of our speakers have addressed personal intimacy with God, stress, leadership development, selecting Bible study materials, keeping a spiritual journal, and mentoring. Bringing in speakers to address our group enriched us in many ways, personally and in our ministry roles.

One meeting centered around "Developing a Three-Minute Testimony." It was facilitated in such a manner that the attendees worked out their own testimonies at the meeting and then were able to return to their respective women's ministries and walk through the process with women on their team. In addition, we began asking an attendee at each subsequent meeting to give her three-minute testimony. This process allowed us to know that woman in a special way—knowing her spiritual journey.

Benefits: We were able to minister to the whole person of the leader. Leaders felt more equipped for ministry because of spiritual growth and good training by competent speakers.

OUR GROWING STEPS

During the next four years our efforts resulted in significant expansion of the ministry and growth of our network.

In 1995 I stepped down as volunteer Director of Women's Ministry at our church and was then free to give more time to the Leaders Group. The group had doubled in size to more than forty women.

Kristin Beasley, Director of the Women's Ministries Department at Phoenix Seminary, a participant of the Leaders Group, shared her vision for a women's ministries conference in June 1996 to be sponsored by the seminary. She invited interested women of the Leaders Group to serve on the conference committee.

This was a great opportunity to represent the organization, work together for a common cause under the direction of the seminary, and encourage leaders to attend the conference, as well as educating the women attending the conference about the Leaders Group.

In 1996 we adopted a new name: LIFT: Leaders In Fellowship Together, and registered our name with the State of Arizona. We chose a hot air balloon to be our logo. In Arizona, where ballooning is common, it visually reflected our mission of giving a lift to our leaders.

We added a new feature to LIFT, a summer workshop that we named "Summertime LIFT." For the first time we charged a fee for an event to cover costs of mailings, the printing of handouts, an honorarium for the speaker, a coffee break and lunch, and hopefully a little left over for the cost of the next meeting's mailing! More than forty women had a wonderful day attending the first Summertime LIFT at a local church to hear Carol Travilla teach on the working styles of women that should be represented on a committee.

Another development in 1996 was modeling and communicating ideas on the how-to's of executing an event for women with transferable ideas so attendees could use them in their own ministry planning, right down to the detail of telling women where we purchased items for lunch, the cost, and how they could order if they desired. We all valued a transferable model.

In 1997 a Day of Prayer was added as a scheduled annual event on our calendar. Our desire was to offer leaders in women's ministry a day for a personal time with God alongside their peers. The day included worship, a devotional, and three blocks of time for personal prayer. Like our other events, the Day of Prayer was hosted by a LIFT member's church and the program planned by the leadership team. This day lived out our belief that prayer is the undergirding of all that we do. Leaders could spend time in personal prayer and also have opportunity to pray with their church ministry teams.

How Would LIFT Stay Relevant?

In order for the leadership team to hear the current issues that women were dealing with in their ministries and to keep LIFT relevant, an advisory board was formed. Three women who attended LIFT on a regular basis and served as volunteer directors of women's ministry at local churches were invited to serve on this board for a one-year term. They met with the leadership team two or three times during this year for consultation and prayer.

There were several benefits to this decision. We listened to these women on the front lines and worked to keep our meetings relevant and meeting expressed needs. Spending time with this group of women developed intimacy and provided them a "small group" that was a safe place to expose their hearts.

In 1998 and 1999 the leadership team, both present and past members, met on several occasions, including a mountain weekend retreat, to fine-tune our mission and goals and vocalize our dreams for LIFT. We spent time discussing the journey of LIFT. We asked ourselves, "What are the current potholes we need to deal with?"

The benefits of these retreat times proved to be many. For example, at the mountain retreat, each woman told her spiritual journey, and that helped to increase understanding and respect for each other. It proved to be a time when we could deepen friendships, listen to each other, pray together, and in the end, with God's help, determine the next part of LIFT's journey.

We decided our mission statement would be: "equipping and encouraging leaders in women's ministries." We would filter all ideas for meetings through this grid by asking, "How does this idea equip and/or encourage leaders in women's ministries?"

To encourage the women leaders in the area to attend the annual April Phoenix Seminary Women's Ministry Conference, we eliminated the April LIFT meeting.

We would continue to meet the first Friday of October, November, February, and March. A Day of Prayer was held in June, and Summertime LIFT was held mid-July.

Benefits: Because of consistency in our meeting schedule, leaders could plan their calendars in advance. We shared in a community ministry outside of our organization.

What Would We Want to Do if We Were Really Dreaming?

If money were not an issue, what would our dreams be for LIFT? We had a great opportunity on that mountain retreat to dream together as we brainstormed and even spent time designing the "perfect" brochure. Our dreams included:

* adding volunteers to the LIFT leadership team

* completing the legal process for LIFT to become a 501 (c) (3) nonprofit organization

* creating sources of funding for publications, teaching materials, and seminars

* having a professional graphic designer create our hot air balloon logo

* designing and printing a "smashing" professional brochure

* growing beyond the Phoenix area

* publishing a regular LIFT newsletter *and someday . . .*

* having the Director of LIFT as a paid position

* working from a LIFT office

A DOCTRINAL POTHOLE

A crisis moment came in 1998 over a particular doctrinal belief held by one of the pastors at a church scheduled to host a LIFT meeting. The pastor of one of our advisory committee members informed her of his concerns over this particular pastor and doctrinal issue. In fact, if the meeting were to be held at that church, her pastor encouraged her not to attend that meeting and to withdraw from LIFT. Our leadership team had to grapple with many questions. Would we refuse women leaders from certain denominations? Would they refuse association with us? Would we accept an invitation to be hosted by any church that invited us?

First we decided to investigate the concern . . .

I consulted with my pastor on how best to do this, and he suggested, "Why don't I just telephone their pastor right now." He spoke with the pastor and found that the former pastor of the church did hold a nontraditional doctrinal belief, but the current pastor did not. My pastor recommended that this was an opportunity for LIFT to decide how inclusive or exclusive we were going to be. He knew that we wanted to adopt a LIFT statement of faith, and he suggested that if we desired to be inclusive then our statement of faith should contain only basic doctrinal nonnegotiables. The leadership team wanted to be inclusive—

all women would be welcomed at a LIFT meeting—but we would only accept invitations to be hosted by churches that agreed with our statement of faith. All women and churches would know up front our doctrinal positions.

This crisis caused us to develop and agree on a written statement of faith. We adopted an abbreviated version of the Statement of Faith of the National Association of Evangelicals. All LIFT attendees would know our doctrinal nonnegotiables.

LIFT STATEMENT OF FAITH

1. We believe the Bible to be the inspired, the only infallible, authoritative Word of God.

2. We believe that there is one God, eternally existent in three persons: Father, Son, and Holy Spirit.

3. We believe in the deity of our Lord Jesus Christ,

> in His virgin birth,

> in His sinless life,

> in His atoning death through His shed blood,

> in His bodily resurrection,

> in His ascension to the right hand of the Father,

> in His personal return in power and glory.

4. We believe in the ministry of the Holy Spirit who convicts, regenerates, baptizes, indwells, enlightens, and empowers believers for godly living.

5. We believe that man was created in the image of God, that he sinned in Adam, and that he is now a sinner by nature and by choice.

6. We believe in salvation by grace through faith in Jesus Christ.

7. We believe in the resurrection of both the saved and the lost:

they that are saved unto the resurrection of life,

they that are lost unto the resurrection of damnation.

8. We believe in the spiritual unity of believers in our Lord Jesus Christ.

Then, 2000-2001 were exciting years. I asked the leadership team to pray the prayer of Jabez (1 Chronicles 4:10) for LIFT. Not knowing what the results would be, we prayed asking God "to bless LIFT indeed, enlarge our territory, that Your hand would be with us, and keep us from evil, that we may not cause pain!"

God answered many of our dreams and even did the unexpected—we "birthed a baby."

✤ In the fall of 2000 a group of women's ministry leaders from Tucson (130 miles south of Phoenix), who occasionally attended LIFT, told me that they would like to begin a "Tucson LIFT." This had been a personal dream of mine for two years, but I had to wait for God's timing. I met with four Tucson leaders, and we agreed on their adopting the LIFT doctrinal and mission statements and becoming a LIFT chapter. They scheduled a leadership coffee at their church to see if ministry leaders were interested. I attended the coffee and explained the vision of LIFT. The Tucson women responded positively. God raised a leadership team for direction, and now Tucson LIFT is beginning its second year of ministry with more than forty participants.

✤ A graphic artist designed our logo, giving us a more polished look.

✤ Legal work for the 501 (c) (3) was completed in December 2001, and we received our final IRS approval on April 17, 2002. What an exciting day! We are celebrating and thanking God for answering our prayers. God continues to be faithful to LIFT. This process, which took several months, was done working with a Christian attorney to ensure that everything was done decently and in order. The cost was $2,500. We knew that we needed to take this step, but where would we get the money? God graciously provided the cost through donations once we took the step by faith! Because of our new nonprofit status, we received several year-end donations. God graciously provided for our monetary needs.

❧ We decided to transition from depending on offerings, which were just covering expenses, to move toward a membership organization. To provide "working capital" for the growing ministry, we made a decision to have a small annual membership fee of $25. Membership benefits include: a roster of LIFT members, speaker referrals, mailings about meetings and resources, and a reduced fee for special seminars. Any woman will be welcomed to attend a LIFT meeting, but only members will receive the stated benefits.

❧ An additional leader with experience as a minister to women at a local church, and as an international speaker and author, joined the LIFT leadership team. She brought her great experience, visionary gift, creativity, and enthusiasm to the team.

❧ Our "smashing," professionally designed membership brochure was ready for distribution at our first meeting of 2002 in February.

By God's direction and blessing we were well on our way to accomplishing most of the goals set in 1998 and 1999.

We believe that 2002 is a year of *new beginnings* for LIFT. God has been faithful and provided each step of the way. It seems that now that we have navigated the journey of LIFT to this point, He is saying— *"It is time for the LIFT-off. It is time to soar!"* We are ready and excited to soar together with Him!

Has it been worth all the work and prayer to get to this point in the journey? Three of our LIFT members explain why they think so:

"LIFT has provided opportunities for me to know what is current and relevant in women's ministries. LIFT has also given me leadership partners upon whom I can rely for advice and prayer. I have found something of value at every LIFT meeting, either for my ministry or for me personally."

> ✐KAREN HARRIS, Director of Women's Ministries, Grace Community Church, Tempe, Arizona

"Like-minded women sharing Inspiration, Friendship and Training says LIFT to me!
Like-minded: having the same ideas, taste, etc.;
Inspiration: a divine influence on human beings;
Friendship: attachment between friends;
Training: to instruct so as to make proficient or qualified."

> ✐MARILYN STUCKWISCH, Director of Women's Ministries, Christ Church-Lutheran, Phoenix, Arizona

"My call to full-time women's ministry service literally occurred at a LIFT meeting. The group has been of great encouragement to my ministry through helping to equip leaders in the unique call of ministering to women. The benefits of fellowship, friendship and networking of LIFT are beyond measure."

> ✐DEBBI DILK, Women's Minister, First Christian Church, Phoenix, Arizona

WHAT ABOUT YOU?

Every leader needs a place to connect with other women in ministry, a place where she can be encouraged and equipped: encouraged in her personal walk with God, and encouraged and equipped for greater effectiveness in her ministry.

Do you as a leader have such a place? If not, I encourage you to take a risk and begin a networking group in your area. I encourage you to take the following steps.

1. Pray for a season to hear God about this idea and how to go about beginning a fellowship of leaders.

2. Invite a few like-minded leaders to meet with you. Even if you know only one, start with one. If you don't know one, ask God to show you one. Propose the idea and begin to pray together.

3. Consider our design framework to evaluate your unique needs and situation; adjust and adapt as God leads you to create a networking group in your area.

4. Contact me if you would like coaching through this process. My address is 9491 E. Voltaire Drive, Scottsdale AZ 85260.

You will be blessed! Remember, every leader needs a LIFT.

Pat Davis has been active in women's ministries for almost twenty-five years, including serving as Director of Women's Ministries in two large churches in the Phoenix area. Presently Pat is the Director of LIFT.: Leaders in Fellowship Together, a networking organization for women's ministry leaders with a mission of "equipping and encouraging leaders in women's ministries."

SPECIAL ENCOURAGEMENT FOR THE PASTOR'S WIFE

Gayle Haggard

In many churches, the pastor's wife is called upon to be the women's ministry leader. If the calling is from the Lord, this experience may be challenging but at the same time wonderfully fulfilling as she steps into the service God has called her to. If, on the other hand, she steps into the role because no one else has or to fulfill the expectations of others, chances are she will quickly be overburdened, stressed out, and stretched way too thin. If you are a pastor's wife, sit back and get ready for some special encouragement from one who has walked in your shoes.

YOU TOO CAN BE FREE:
SECRETS OF A HAPPY PASTOR'S WIFE

When I think of being happy, I imagine the woman in Proverbs 31 who smiles at the future. She seems to have a substantive contentment, maybe even a few secrets tucked away in her heart that give her strength to face life with joy. I want to be like her in this; in fact, I think I am. And I am a happy pastor's wife.

I hope that's not an oxymoron. However, many pastors' wives tell me that they are not happy. In fact a friend just called this morning to tell me about a meeting she had recently with three pastors' wives who were feeling out of place in their roles in the church. They felt they were just not cut out for being pastors' wives and could not live up to the expectations that went along with it.

It reminded me of the discussion I had with my mother many years ago when I was seventeen years old, a senior in high school. I remember leaning across the counter, resting on my hands, with a dreamy look in my eyes and saying, "I think I would like to be married to a pastor someday." My mother responded with, "But, Gayle, you don't play the piano or sing." That had not occurred to me. Did a pastor's wife really have to do those things? I wondered if there really were prerequisites to being a pastor's wife that set her apart from other Christian wives.

Amazingly, several years later, I did fall in love with a man whom God had called to be a pastor. Here I am, almost thirty years later, thinking this is indeed a wonderful life. And the secrets I've found are really no different from those of other Christian wives. I've learned to sincerely love God and to sincerely love my husband and children. Beyond that, I try to live my life in obedience to God and, it's true, oblivious to the expectation of others. Shouldn't this be true of all of us?

"What?" you ask. "What about all the expectations of the people in our churches?" Are they the controlling factors in our lives? In order to lead responsibly beside our husbands, we have to be free to obey

God and to live according to His Word. We can't do this if we are bound up with the expectations of others. Doing so will drain us and ultimately burn us out.

In their exhortational book *Married to a Pastor,* authors H. B. London and Neil B. Wiseman write about the expectations on pastors' wives. In their chapter "I Hate the E Word," they point out that many pastors' wives are overly weary of unrealistic expectations and state that "expectations are a gigantic problem for ministers' mates. Horror stories abound about wives with too much to do, too many people to please and too many burdens to bear."[1]

Certainly some expectations are in keeping with biblical instruction and should be adhered to. As pastors' wives, we should live lives worthy of respect. But this is true for all Christian women. We do this out of our love for God, to be a help to our husbands, and to be a blessing and an encouragement for all who are watching. It has nothing to do with the unbiblical overscrutinizing of the few who want to control us and make our lives miserable. We are in a position to graciously and purposely set an example of godliness that other women can follow. This is leadership and others will respect it. If we give in to the unbiblical expectations of others, we become overburdened and weak. If we hold our ground in doing the things we know God has given us to do with graciousness and strength of heart, then we grow stronger in the eyes of others and better able to lead.

Loving Our Husbands

And leadership is something God has called us to, alongside our husbands. We are one with them and share in their callings. I am not talking about competing with them in their pastoral roles. I'm talking about completing them and helping them, sharing in their work, and being strength to their lives. Remember, men bond with the women who help them. We need to be those women in our husbands' lives.

First Corinthians 11:7 says that woman is the glory of man. Proverbs 12:4 says, "A wife of noble character is her husband's crown." That is what I want to be to my husband. I want to be a glory to him. I want him to feel that having me makes him look good. I can't do this if I hate my role. So it's up to me to shape my role in a way that is pleasing to God, helpful to my husband, and a joy to me.

I'll never forget the time I was giving a presentation to a group of local pastors in our city about a project I cared very much about. Before going in to the meeting I prayed that God would help me to speak clearly, graciously, and intelligently to these men so I wouldn't be an embarrassment to my husband. As I spoke, out of the corner of my eye I could see him glowing. God answered my prayer and enabled me to speak well. In those few moments I was a glory to my husband. Afterward he walked me to the car and hugged me tightly before I left. What is that worth? It motivated me to look for other ways to be a glory to my husband.

Of course each of us is unique, and we can be a glory to our husbands in a variety of ways. These ways will also vary as we go through the different seasons of our lives. For many years I focused my ministry on my husband and children. I felt one with my husband in his ministry, but felt that the best way I could serve him and our church was by taking care of him and our children. Our church learned to expect this from me, and I felt supported in this all-important role. I even had women write me letters thanking me for setting an example in the way I was loving my husband and children. They said it freed them to do the same. Understand, I was still visible. I loved our church and thoroughly enjoyed being a part of it. I just didn't take on responsibilities that were beyond what I could do well.

Ministry in the Church

As time passed, my children grew older, and I felt God leading me to take on new responsibilities, such as our women's ministry and coordinating the National Day of Prayer event for our city. But these were God-given callings, not expectation-fulfilling burdens. In whatever God calls us to do, He gives us the strength and joy to do it. Remember His yoke is easy and His burden light (Matthew 11:30).

For many years we did not have a women's ministry, at least not as extensive as some thought a church our size should have. We had a couple of small Bible studies taught by women, but that was the extent of it. In due time, however, God laid it on my heart to develop our women's ministry. It is a great blessing to our church now to have this, but we were a growing, thriving church before we had it. My husband used to say that we are not a full-service church, meaning that we didn't offer every kind of ministry that could be offered. However, over time God has raised up people in our congregation and added people to us to take on more areas of ministry. We didn't try to do everything. We did what we could and what we felt God had given us to do, and eventually God added others to do more. This has significance for the pastor's wife in that she shouldn't try to do everything herself just because no one else is doing it. There is joy in doing what we know God has given to us; doing more sometimes becomes a burden. Of course the pastor's wife needs to be considerate of what her husband asks her to do. It is her role to help him. But perhaps together they should consider what is really necessary.

Once I received a letter from a woman thanking me for not trying to fill all of the traditional pastor's wife roles in the church. It allowed others with special giftings to serve in those roles. That set me free and gave me confidence I was on the right track.

Being a pastor's wife shouldn't be a burden; rather, it should be an honor. As I stated earlier, our God-given expectations are the same as those for any Christian wife. However, we are also given influence. If we step into this role willingly, graciously, and with strength and wisdom, we can play a powerful role alongside our husbands in loving and serving the body of Christ and helping to bring it to maturity. If we choose to succumb to the burdensome expectations of others, we may burn out and not have the strength to use our influence for any good. It's time pastors' wives shake the image of the poor, overburdened woman living in a fishbowl and become set free to shape their lives and their service in a way that is pleasing to God, a blessing to their husbands and families, and a joy to themselves. I would say that's reason to smile at the future.

Gayle Haggard is the wife of Ted Haggard, who pastors New Life Church, a seven-thousand-member congregation located in Colorado Springs. As Director of Women's Ministry, Gayle helps lead more than one hundred small groups in genuinely knowing the Lord and discovering the strength they can bring to the body of Christ as mature, godly women.

[1] H. B. London and Neil B. Wiseman, *Married to a Pastor* (Ventura, Calif.: Regal, 1999), 117.

WHY WE DO
WHAT WE DO

Lysa TerKeurst

I was exhausted. All I wanted to do was to get to my assigned seat on the plane and settle in for a long winter's nap. Imagine my absolute delight at being the only person seated in my row. I was praising the Lord and just about to close my eyes when two last-minute passengers made their way to my row and took their seats.

Reluctantly, I decided to forgo my nap. The last thing I needed was to fall asleep and snore or worse yet wake up with my head resting on the shoulder of the guy beside me. No, I didn't need another most embarrassing moment, so I pulled this book's manuscript out of my bag and started working.

"What are you working on?" the man beside me inquired. I told him I was a writer and this book's title was going to be

"Leading Women to the Heart of God." He smiled and informed me that he thought God was a very interesting topic. I agreed and asked him a few questions about his beliefs, and before long I found myself telling my entire testimony. I reached into my bag and pulled out my Bible and walked him through some key verses that dealt with some of the issues he was facing in his life. He kept asking questions, and I kept praying that God would give me answers.

Needless to say, I was no longer tired at all. The excitement of discussing my faith had my mind reeling and my mind racing. All of a sudden I felt God tugging at my heart to give this man my Bible. Now this was not just any Bible; this was my everyday, highlighted, underlined, written-in, and tearstained Bible. I started to argue with God in my head, but it was clear, I was to give away my Bible.

I emptied it of some old church bulletins and other papers tucked throughout, took a deep breath, sighed, and placed the Bible on his lap. "I'd like for you to have my Bible," I said. Astonished, the man started to hand the Bible back to me, saying he couldn't possibly accept such a gift. I insisted and said that in fact God had instructed me to give him my Bible. I told him that sometimes the God of the universe pauses in the midst of all of His creation to touch the heart of one person, and today God paused for him.

The man took the Bible and made two promises to me. He said he would read this Bible and then someday he would pass it on, doing for someone else what I'd done for him. Before I knew it, the plane landed, and as it taxied to the gate the woman sitting on the other side of the man reached across him and grabbed my arm. "You have transformed my life today," she said as tears steamed down her cheeks. "What you shared makes so much sense. I will never be the same. Thank you."

I was in absolute awe at what God allowed me to take part in that day. God allowed me to join Him in His work, and it was awesome.

Several minutes after exiting the plane I was weaving in and out of the crowds trying to find my gate when I spotted the man from the plane. He stopped me to once again thank me and to tell me that he had been praying to God. We swapped business cards, and I asked him to keep in touch.

About a month later he called to tell me that his life had totally changed. He'd taken a week off from work to read the Bible, and he'd already shared his testimony with more than one hundred people. He also told me that after reading the Scriptures he knew he needed to get involved in a church, so he'd decided to visit a large church in town. On his way there he passed another church, and a strong feeling came over him that he was to turn his car around and go back to that church. So he did. When he got to his seat in the sanctuary, he opened up his bulletin and gasped. Inside the bulletin he saw my picture and an announcement that I was to be the speaker at an upcoming ladies conference. He said he felt that, once again, God had paused just for him, and he's been attending that church ever since.

This is why we do what we do, to reach others for Christ. Men and women, young and old, rich and poor, they all need Jesus Christ. My whole conversation with this man started because he saw the title of this book. My prayer all along has been that God would use this book to start a revival. Isn't it exciting to see God answer prayer and transform lives right before our very eyes? Oh, how I pray, my dear friend, that God would use you in a mighty way and that He would use this book to encourage and equip you for the exciting journey ahead. Let's keep our eyes fixed on Jesus, stay faithful to the course set before us, and take great joy in leading women to the heart of God.

Lysa TerKeurst is a wife, mother of three daughters, and President of Proverbs 31 Ministries. She has been featured on *The 700 Club, Focus on the Family, How to Manage Your Money* with Larry Burkett, and Billy Graham's *Decision Today* radio program. Lysa is one of the voices behind the Proverbs 31 radio program heard daily from coast to coast. She has also written *Seven Life Principles for Every Woman*, *Who Holds the Key to Your Heart?*, *Living Life on Purpose*, *Capture Her Heart* (for husbands), and *Capture His Heart* (for wives). Lysa is also an inspirational speaker for women's events and marriage conferences throughout the country.

YOU ARE NOT ALONE: MINISTRIES THAT CAN COME ALONGSIDE YOU

Lou Ann McClendon

A church women's ministry can be everything God has designed it to be; there is no reason for it to be anything less than what the Lord has planned! When the three key pieces are in place—God, the willing servant-leader, and women—there is no limit to the exciting, life-changing experiences that can come out of a church women's ministry. We know that our heavenly Father supplies the love, power, wisdom, and truth. We know that women will bring a variety of issues and needs to the table. God has called the servant-leader to seek Him and serve His precious daughters.

The shape and form of the women's ministry in any given local church should be uniquely designed to meet the needs of the special women God has called to that church, and will be delivered through the gifts and anointing of the chosen leaders. In many of the chapters within this book, experienced women's ministry leaders have suggested a variety of ways and means of going about the process of developing a vibrant ministry. Here is a "guide-at-a-glance" to working with God to find His plan for *your* women's ministry and to discover how to access the many ministry resources He has placed within the body of Christ.

PRAY AND SEEK

God has called you to your position of service and influence. He will also supply you with guidance and insight into how to reach out to women with His love and grace. Never, ever, skip this step!

OBSERVE AND INQUIRE

Spend time really studying the women in your group. Ask God for knowledge into their true heart issues and needs. Look not only at the active participants but at the "invisible" women—the ones who attend services but are not currently involved in your existing programs.

IDENTIFY AND DEVELOP THE LEADERS

Let God show you those whom He has called to join you in your labors and support you in prayer. Recognize gifts and callings, and bring them into your process. Many hands make the work light!

PLAN AND STRATEGIZE

This is where activities and programs can actually meet the felt needs of women. Don't be content to just "do it" the way it has always been done. What will bring the women you know into a deeper walk with the Lord? What will grow them beyond themselves into greater service to their families, church, communities, culture, and beyond?

TAP INTO RESOURCE
MINISTRIES IN THE BODY OF CHRIST

God has raised up a large number and variety of ministries that can help you reach women effectively. As you pursue the Lord's plan for your church, consider the following ministries and the possible ways they can provide support for your purposes. As your ministry grows, you may find you must reach out to increasingly diverse groups of women. Review the partial list below for excellent programming resources to help meet the challenges and accomplish your goals. Keep in mind that this is not a complete listing of the multitude of ministries available.

Focus on the Family provides quality resources to promote emotional and spiritual health, dynamic family relationships, and creative parenting, among others. Mastering the multimedia channels of print, radio, audio theater, and video, Focus has developed challenging and entertaining resources to help raise a godly family.

> Focus on the Family
> James C. Dobson, Ph.D., President
> Colorado Springs, CO 80995
> Office: (719) 531-3400
> Toll Free: (800) A-FAMILY (232-6459)
> Facsimile: (719) 531-3424
> www.family.org

Renewing the Heart Women's Ministries, a ministry of Focus on the Family, exists to equip women with biblical principles and practical tools, encouraging and challenging them to pattern their lives not after the world but after the Word of God. Tune in on Saturdays (1:00 P.M. EST in most areas) to Renewing the Heart's live call-in radio broadcast, and join host Janet Parshall as she discusses women's issues with listeners from around the country. Check out renewingtheheart.com for articles on women's issues, tips for life, true stories about women around the world, and ideas about ways you can affect your culture for the kingdom of God. Join the Renewing the Heart team as they pursue the goal of equipping and encouraging women's ministry leaders to do the work of the gospel.

> Renewing the Heart
> Yvette Maher, Vice President
> P.O. Box 670
> Colorado Springs, CO 80901-0670
> Office: (719) 548-5750
> Facsimile: (719) 548-4667
> www.renewingtheheart.com

Proverbs 31 Ministries is dedicated to glorifying God by touching women's hearts to build godly homes. Through Jesus Christ, Proverbs 31 sheds light on the Lord's distinctive design for women and the great responsibilities they have been given. With Proverbs 31:10–31 as a guide, the ministry encourages and equips women to practice the seven principles of the Proverbs 31 woman. Books, "The P31 Woman" monthly newsletter, a Website, radio broadcasts, and chartered Encouragement Groups are a few of the channels used by Proverbs 31 Ministries to inspire and encourage women. Proverbs 31 also has dynamic speakers available for church conferences and retreats.

> Proverbs 31 Ministries
> Lysa TerKeurst

616–G Matthews—Mint Hill Road
Matthews, NC 28105
Office: (704) 849-2270
Toll Free: (877) 731-4663
Facsimile: (704) 849-7267
www.Proverbs31.org

Mothers of Preschoolers (MOPS International, Inc.) recognizes that the years from infancy to kindergarten are foundational in a mother-child relationship and are filled with unique needs. MOPS exists to meet the needs of *every* mom—urban and suburban moms, stay-at-home and working moms, teen, single, and married moms—moms with different lifestyles who all share a similar desire to be the very best moms they can be! A MOPS group grows a church through leadership development and outreach into the community. Find out how to have a MOPS group in your church!

Mothers of Preschoolers (MOPS International, Inc.)
Carol Kuykendall, Director of Communications
1311 S. Clarkson Street
P.O. Box 102200
Denver, CO 80250-2200
Office: (303) 733-5353
Toll Free: (800) 929-1287
Facsimile: (303) 733-5770
www.mops.org

Precept Ministries is a transdenominational organization dedicated to the sole purpose of teaching people to study God's Word for themselves and to apply its truths to their daily lives. This is achieved through the inductive study method, a highly effective way of seeking out answers and understanding Scripture. Through thought-provoking materials, radio and television programs, study tours to the Holy Land, and conferences and camps for men, women, teens, and college students, Precept is working to establish people in God's Word all over the world.

Precept Ministries
Jack and Kay Arthur, Chief Executive Officers
7324 Noah Reid Road
P.O. Box 182218
Chattanooga, TN 37422
Office: (423) 892-6814
Toll Free: (800) 763-8280
www.precept.org

Apples of Gold is a six-week mentoring program based on Titus 2:3–5. Each week a different mentor facilitates the activities, which include one hour of cooking, one hour of Bible study based on Titus 2:3–5, and a fellowship hour spent enjoying the food that has been prepared. Lessons provide the guidelines for mentors to share biblical wisdom as well as personal experiences to nurture and train younger participants. The book *Apples of Gold* is a complete guide for starting the program in your church or neighborhood. *Gifts of Gold* is a supplemental book offering additional ideas and tested tips from hundreds of established classes. *Appleseeds* is a ten-week mentoring program for pre-teen girls that includes Bible lessons, manners education, and craft ideas to reinforce the lesson.

Apples of Gold
Betty Huizenga
1298 Waukazoo Drive
Holland, MI 49424
Office: (616) 399-4001
www.applesofgold.org

Hearts At Home is a nondenominational, Christ-centered professional organization founded to encourage and educate mothers at home or those who want to be. Hearts At Home uses conferences, magazines, devotionals, a Website, and referrals to help moms understand their God-given value and the important role they play in society.

> Hearts At Home
> Jill Savage, Founder
> 900 W. College Avenue
> Normal, IL 61761
> Office: (309) 888-MOMS
> Facsimile: (309) 888-4525
> www.hearts-at-home.org

Crown Financial Ministries is committed to providing Scripture-based fiscal wisdom, money management training, and practical tools to 5 percent of the world's population in the next fifteen years. Using broadcasting, Internet, and print publications, they offer sound advice and instruction to every age group across many national barriers. Single or married, young or old, check out their Website to find out how to get out of debt, send your kids to college, retire reasonably, *and* finance the spread of the gospel!

> Crown Financial Ministries
> Howard Dayton, CEO
> P.O. Box 100
> Gainesville, GA 30503-0100
> Office: (770) 534-1000
> www.crown.org

CLASS has grown into a complete service agency for the established and aspiring Christian speaker, author, and publisher. Focusing on the

Christian community, CLASS finds raw talent, trains it, develops it, educates it, and nurtures it, and when it is ready, launches it through their speaker service and publishing assistance. Churches and other Christian groups from all over the country call CLASS looking for speakers for various events. Need a speaker? Give CLASS a call.

> CLASS
> Marita Littauer, President
> P.O. Box 66810
> Albuquerque, NM 87193-6810
> Office: (800) 433-6633
> Facsimile: (505) 899-9282
> www.classervices.com

Sisters in Service is the Women's Ministry division of Partners International, a global ministry that works to create partnerships with God's people in the least Christian regions of the world. Sisters in Service invites women (largely American) to adopt—relationally, financially, and prayerfully—some of the 2,500 indigenous women embraced and supported by Sisters as they minister to unreached women and children in some of the poorest countries around the world. American women's lives have been transformed as they expanded their personal territory to include relationships with and support of these valiant sisters serving the kingdom of God. Consider sponsoring a chapter of Sisters in Service in your church.

> Sisters in Service
> c/o Partners International
> 1313 N. Atlantic Avenue, Suite 4000
> Spokane, WA 99201
> Office: (509) 343-4000
> Toll Free: (800) 966-5515

Facsimile: (509) 343-4015
www.partnersintl.org
www.sistersinservice.org

N.E.W. Ministries is committed to the spiritual growth and emotional well-being of women who are going through the transition and adjustment of moving. *After the Boxes Are Unpacked* takes a woman through the process of letting go, starting over, and moving ahead with her life while keeping her focus on Christ. The book, teacher's manual, newcomer's workbook, and video series provide all the tools necessary to gather a group of newcomers together, knit them into your body, and release them into service. This is a must for churches in today's transient communities.

N.E.W. Ministries
Susan Miller, President
P.O. Box 5692
Scottsdale, AZ 85261-5692
Office: (480) 991-5268
Toll Free: (866) 587-8668
Facsimile: (480) 998-9802
www.justmoved.org

Concerned Women for America is the nation's largest public policy women's organization with a rich twenty-two-year history of helping CWA members across the country bring biblical principles into all levels of public policy. Built on prayer and action, CWA desires to protect and promote biblical values among all citizens by influencing society and reversing the decline in moral values in our nation. CWA covets your participation and can provide educational and organizational resources for your women.

Concerned Women for America
1015 Fifteenth Street N.W., Suite 1100
Washington, DC 20005
Office: (202) 488-7000
Facsimile: (202) 488-0806
www.cwfa.org

Crisis Pregnancy Ministry exists to encourage, extend, and support the work being done by pregnancy resource centers across the nation. Statistics show that one out of every six abortions are performed on women who consider themselves evangelical Christians. Pregnancy resource centers are on the front lines in most communities, making a practical, loving effort to help women choose life over abortion and to minister God's forgiveness and healing to women devastated by past abortion decisions. Special Bible studies designed to bring about reconciliation and restoration are available for the wounded in your midst. Let women know that there is help and freedom from the shame of the sins of the past. You can contact Crisis Pregnancy Ministry to find the location of a pregnancy resource center, learn how women can serve in a local crisis pregnancy center, or learn how to begin a facility in your area.

Crisis Pregnancy Ministry
Julie Parton, Manager
c/o Focus on the Family
8605 Explorer Drive
Colorado Springs, CO 80920
Office: (719) 531-3460
Facsimile: (719) 548-4667
www.thinkaboutitonline.com
www.family.org/pregnancy

LifeWay Christian Resources publishes Bible-based resources for women's ministry programming and strategies. Check out their colorful catalogue for materials to enhance your leadership training, Bible studies, and small group activities (including the Beth Moore and Anne Graham Lotz studies), and for events designed to lead you and your group of women into a deeper walk with the Lord. LifeWay's many diverse materials are sure to help address the varied needs of your women's ministry.

> LifeWay Christian Resources
> of the Southern Baptist Convention
> One LifeWay Plaza
> Nashville, TN 37234
> Office: (800) 458-2772
> www.lifeway.com

Women's Ministries at Multnomah Bible College and Seminary, a pioneer in the educational field of Women's Ministries, offers both a four-year Bachelor's degree and a two-year Master's degree in Women's Ministries. Additionally, Multnomah conducts an annual "Women in Ministry" conference, which is designed to educate and equip women from all over the United States in their ministry leadership roles.

> Multnomah Women's Ministries
> Multnomah Bible College:
> Prof. Bonnie S. Kopp, Chair
> Multnomah Biblical Seminary:
> Prof. Valerie Clemen, Chair
> 8435 N.E. Glisan Street
> Portland, OR 97220

Admissions: (800) 275-4672
Local: (503) 251-6485
www.multnomah.edu

Women in Ministry Conference
Development Department (503) 251-6594

Sonlife Ministries offers quality training in disciple making for small groups, church leaders, women in ministry, and youth leaders. Sonlife has a heart for Growing Healthy Women in Ministry and has scheduled strategy seminars: Disciplemaking Ministry as Modeled by Jesus throughout the country. Advanced training is also available to help you with balance, vision, and multiplication, bringing health to every dimension of your disciple-making church.

Sonlife Ministries
Jean Milliken, National Women in Ministry Director
526 N. Main
Elburn, IL 60119
Office: (630) 365-5855
Facsimile: (630) 365-5892
www.sonlife.com

Embracing Womanhood Project is committed to empowering young women and equipping leaders through foundational biblical teaching to embrace God's purposeful design of womanhood in a contemporary culture. This purpose is carried out by providing Live the Difference conferences, leadership training, speaking engagements, college forums and debates, and strategic ministry projects. By influencing young women and building tomorrow's leaders, the project endeavors to profoundly affect the next generation for the sake of the kingdom.

Embracing Womanhood Project
Cheri Jimenez, President
206 New Bern Place
Raleigh, NC 27601
Office: (866) EWP-LIVE or (866) 397-5483
Facsimile: (919) 831-1122
cjimenez@embracingwomanhood.org

Lou Ann McClendon, Manager of Renewing the Heart Women's Ministries at Focus on the Family, has been married for twenty-seven years and is grateful for and proud of her three "mostly grown" children. Lou Ann has served as Coordinator of Women's Ministry in her church, written a women's Bible study, spoken at women's retreats, and led many women's Bible study small groups. Her heart's desire is to see women fully healed and freed from past hurts and bondage, in order to fully walk in God's love and the calling He has for each of His daughters.

renewing the heart®

Truth and Grace for Daily Living

Welcome to a Special Place Just for Women

We hope you've enjoyed this book.
Renewing the Heart, a ministry of Focus on the Family,
is dedicated to equipping and encouraging women in all facets
of their lives. Through our weekly call-in radio program,
our Web site, and a variety of other outreaches,
Renewing the Heart is a place to find answers, gain support,
and, most of all, know you're among friends.

How to Reach Us

For more information and additional resources, visit our Web site
at www.renewingtheheart.com. Here, you'll find articles,
devotions, and broadcast information on our weekly call-in
radio program, "Renewing the Heart," hosted by Janet Parshall.

To request any of these resources, call Focus on the Family at
800-A-FAMILY (800-232-6459). In Canada, call 800-661-9800.

You may also write us at:
Focus on the Family, Colorado Springs, CO 80995

In Canada, write to: Focus on the Family,
P.O. Box 9800, Stn. Terminal, Vancouver, B.C. V6B 4G3

To learn more about Focus on the Family or to find out if we have
an associate office in your country, please visit www.family.org.

We'd love to hear from you!

Another Great Title from Lysa TerKeurst and Moody Press

Who Holds the Key to Your Heart

Have you wished for a life full of love, joy and peace but haven't known where to find it? Have you ever felt haunted by the hurts from your past?

Inside each of us lies a secret place, hidden from the view of outsiders. We live in fear and shame of anyone venturing too close to our secrets; our discontentment of what could have been, doubt, insecurity, bitterness and addiction. We cannot escape Satan's aim to keep us prisoner to our sins by using our own knowledge and strength.

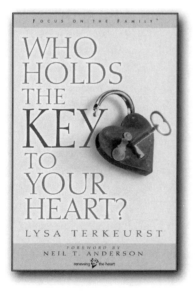

The truth is God knows the secrets of your heart and He is waiting for you to give them to Him. He wants the key to your heart, your whole heart—especially the hidden parts.

Who Hold the Key to Your Heart? is your map through the deepest places of your soul, where God can reveal His truth and set you free. Once He unlocks every hurting and dark place, He will then offer you hope, heal you with God's Word and fill you with His redeeming love, joy and peace!

ISBN: 0-8024-3310-3

MOODY
The Name You Can Trust
1-800-678-8812 **www.MoodyPress.org**

Moody Press, a ministry of Moody Bible Institute,
is designed for education, evangelization, and edification.
If we may assist you in knowing more about Christ
and the Christian life, please write us without obligation:
Moody Press, c/o MLM, Chicago, Illinois 60610.